Total Perception

(Book 1)

Sadguru Swami Shivdas

Eyes cannot perceive what the Mind does not conceive.

Barriers to Total Perception

Our Delusion 1

Time 9

Separation 19

Logical Reasoning 31

Denying Reality 43

Misuse of Energy 53

Dependence on Knowledge 59

Stuck with the Past 65

Questions & Challenges 71

Need of Safety 75

Unaware of Change 81

Dropping Out Early 85

Poor Judgment 89

Our Limitations 93

Blind Following 97

The Dual Mistake 103

Security 107

The Maya 111

Ego 115

Impatience 119

Stubbornness 123

Preface

You cannot perceive intentionally. It is not in your power. You can only stop perceiving. You can shut your eyes and stop seeing. You can shut your ears and stop hearing. You can block your nose and stop smelling. You have the power to stop perceiving, but not to start perceiving. Once you have your eyes, nose, ears, or sense organs unblocked, you perceive.

Sensory perceiving is basic to all organisms. There is nothing great about being humans as far as power of perceiving is concerned because every creature has power to perceive. Some can only sense through touch and some can sense touch and smell but any creature however small and insignificant it might seem, have at least one form of sensing its surroundings. Perceiving is the basis of life. In absence of ability to perceive, there is no life.

Being human means something extraordinary. It means to be able to perceive beyond any other form of life around us. It means to be able to perceive totally, completely. But we rarely do so. We can hardly do so. Not only it is not in our power to be able to perceive totally, but we are also so much occupied in our busy lives, that we are hardly aware of our surroundings or our lives.

The only way to be able to perceive totally and therefore experience this universe in a way unimaginable in our present way of living, is to drop all those things that block our senses. Only when we unblock our channels, the perception can happen so completely that we will never ever go back to the dark dungeons of ignorance and unawareness. This book lists out all those blockages that prevent total perception.

Our Delusion

We are the smartest, most capable of species on the planet, yet we cannot compete with any other creature in the sense of perception.

It seems dogs can listen to the sounds that we humans cannot. The range of frequencies that they can hear is about twice that of humans. This means that if a sound is made in the ultrasonic range, the dogs or cats would know of it, but we would not. Instead, we will experience a complete silence if there was no other sound around us. If we talk only about humans, there are hardly a few who can listen even about half of what our ears must be capable of. Then there are some birds like bats or owls who can move around in complete darkness. They do not need the vision of eyes to ascertain the terrain of their path. They use the ability to respond to the reflected sound to know where they are going. As for us, we are completely helpless in absence of a light source, because we depend on our eyes to figure out the physical world around us in order to move about.

We are known to have five major senses to help us experience the universe. These are the senses of vision, hearing, smell, taste, and touch. Those who are more fastidious, would say that we also have the sense of balance, pain, temperature, and proprioception. Proprioception is the ability to know spatial location of our body parts. That is quite a range of perceptions, yet most of our conscious life goes by using just the eyes and the ears. Our fascination with our intellectual ability to respond with our universe works sufficiently well with just the audio and visual components of our perceptions. When it comes to the ability to smell, we perform very poorly. Almost all the other species outsmart us in using their sense of smell to identify food or to detect danger. We are so pathetic in our sense of smell that we cannot figure out what is edible and what is not. At times, we end up finding that our stomach is more intelligent than our nose or tongue to figure out if the food we ate was bad.

In our wakeful state, we experience a universe around us. This universe is made mystical by countless objects and species moving about with certain predictability and a lot of randomness. In the quest to survive for as long as feasible in this world, every living creature explores its opportunities and threats. These opportunities could either be about finding food for survival or any of other hundreds of ways in which pleasure and comfort could be achieved. Yet, in this game of life, the opportunities do not come free. They cannot be availed without avoiding numerous threats which could cause pain, suffering, or death. Each living creature is programmed to avoid danger and pain while pursuing pleasure and growth for itself and its loved ones. The sense organs play an important role in keeping all the living entities moving around enjoying the game of life where some win and the others lose at each moment. We humans are the luckiest of all, because we are equipped with the most sense organs headed by a fully developed brain which we utilize to optimally use our sense organs to our best advantages. It is the brain, not the sense organs which allows a creature to perceive the world in the best manner. The sense organs are just communicators; they pick the signals from environment and transmit to the brain. If the brain is not capable of understanding the thousands of signals received from the sense organs, there is no real advantage of having advanced senses.

It is evident that only those species could have thrived on the planet among countless threats and opportunities who had taken the best advantage of their sense of perception to ascertain their surroundings. Though humans did not have the best sensing capabilities to compete among other creatures, they had a superior brain which could store and process large amount of information. Humans exploited the capabilities of their brains and took control of the planet by overpowering every other form of life. Currently our planet is seen by humans as their home and everything else as the resource to be used and exploited for the betterment of humans only.

In our quest to exist and grow on the planet, we used our survival instinct and made use of our brain to utilize our senses in such a manner that we could use them in the most productive manner. We ascertained every new incident with the help of our accumulated experience from our ancestors and continued to survive by way of innovation and industrialization. This is where we lost touch with the Reality. Though, we had started long back motivated by our survival instincts and a will to

We continue to exist in the survival mode, grabbing the first available opportunity for our pleasure and fearing every little danger as a threat to our survival.

proliferate against our competition with various creatures, at this time we do not realize that we do not need to do that anymore. We have developed our lifestyle so much in contrast to the ancient humans that we do not need to continue working on our survival instincts the way we had to exist several centuries back. We have crossed that bridge long ago. Yet, driven by our habitual way of living this way for thousands of years, we continue to exist in a survival mode, grabbing the first available opportunity for pleasure and fearing every little danger as a threat to our survival.

> *Sheila asked Minal, "Does your five-year-old son still suck his thumb?" Minal said, "Not anymore." Sheila was surprised. She asked if she had taken him to some doctor. Minal said, "No, actually I loosened his pants."*

When one exists in survival mode, one is cautious every moment. In caution, one treats everything as a threat. It could be even a resistance or difference of opinion that could be seen as a threat. When one feels threatened or when in fear, one cannot perceive as one should, one cannot behave as one does. A perception can happen completely only when one is free of thoughts of fear, threat, or concern of any kind. Existing in survival mode also means that one is always chasing pleasures and desires. This endless quest for achieving and acquiring does not let the sense organs and the mind to be open to perceiving. They just perceive enough to survive. Pathetically, survival is the only thought humans have in their minds.

We encounter sensory information in millions of forms every day. Yet, our mind is able to cope with this vast information overload very easily. Since it cannot pay attention to all the available information in a short time, the mind combines all the information as one chunk. It not only integrates a large group of similar information it collects from the sense organs, but it also continues to differentiate any change that it finds in the data as the time progresses. *Essentially, the mind sees that which is changing as a foreground over that which does not change as the background.* This way, driven by the unique capabilities of our minds, we are able to notice only the changes in our environment, not the complete information at any time. Any information that does not change, is simply ignored. We continue to remove all unimportant data while noticing and registering the changes moment after moment, day after day. While we continue to do that, the amount of information in our surrounding which is different from all the past information we have known and collected so far continues to diminish. This leads to less and less information made available to us to pay attention to with every passing moment. Continuing this way, within a few years, most of us are left with a brain that hardly ever comes across a new information. We all have enough information in our brains to allow us to survive all future moments using our experiences. Sadly, our

Figure 1: The brain ignores countless dots. It simply notices two symbols as foreground and everything else as background. Moreover, the two symbols are also not seen as a one and a six, but as a combination, identified as a sixteen.

experience is nothing but the collection of information we have gathered all our life. This way, our sense of perception continues to diminish and by the time we reach the age of sixteen years, we have successfully transformed our intelligent personality into a dumb machine. In such a mechanical way of living life, we are hardly receptive to any new and fresh sensation. We find refuge in utilizing our stored experience instead of experiencing a fresh encounter with the universe. The reason is simple; we are not able to let go our fears and survival instincts. We fear anything new and fresh because new means uncertainty, and security is only in something that is certain, repeatable, and routine. In a hope for living a secured life, we have killed our senses of perception long time back.

Yes, we have killed our senses of perception! It is not an exaggeration. It is truth in its ugly form. We do not see what is available to our eyes or listen what is spoken to us. We see only what is convenient. We see only what we want to see. We see only what we are used to seeing. This applies to all our senses, not just eyes. We hear what is convenient and suits us. We smell and taste in the same distorted manner. If I have grown up as a vegan or a vegetarian all my life, I cannot stand the smell of meat or seafood. Having brought-up such, if I put something new for the first time in my mouth, it does not matter how tasty that might be to most people, I might not like it. Our brains are habitual of liking or disliking based on their past experiences. In experiencing something completely new and fresh, our brains are helpless.

We have developed so much. We have grown so much. We are proud to possess the best mind, supported by the best set of senses when seen in totality. We have a mysterious universe surrounding us which we can become aware of in its totality and its full majesty. We can! If only we were able to perceive the immense beauty and magic surrounding us. If only our eyes could see the beauty in its raw form and not what it was comfortable in seeing! If only our ears could hear

Essentially, the mind sees that which is changing as a foreground over that which does not change as the background.

every fresh sound, and not just what we found comfort hearing in! If only, we could taste and smell everything in its complete innocence and not be conditioned by our past learning and experience! If only we could exist in this magical world ecstatically and not dragged ourselves with burdens of fears and anxieties of an uncertain future and a painful past! If only we could perceive in totality! If that were ever possible, humans would have stopped thinking about Gods, praying them, fighting for them! Instead, they themselves would had come much closer to God.

Throughout this book, we will discuss all the ways in which we have gone far from perceiving reality in its true form. As we start unearthing our behavior and our habits closely, we should be getting a feel of how much we have drifted away from our true nature. Our true nature is not very far from us. It is still very much within us. The only difficulty is that it is hidden too deep under the layers of our conditioning. We could get to it if we truly desired so. The remedy of any problem starts with identification of the problem. A problem is half solved the moment it is recognized as a problem. We too, would possibly come much closer to improving our perceptibility if we could see our blindfolds and bondages. It is not our inability to perceive completely or totally that is difficult. Instead, what is difficult is our inability to identify this fact.

> *A Total Perception is only possible when*
> 1. *We drop our habit to exist in survival mode (Chasing Happiness and Avoiding Pain).*
> 2. *We drop fear of that which is new and uncertain.*
> 3. *We face opposing point of view in the same way as we face approvals and acceptance.*
> 4. *We observe without memory.*
> 5. *We observe only with our senses, not our brain.*

Time

Our enslavement to 'time' does not allow us to perceive in totality.

We exist in time and cannot imagine anything outside the realm of time. From our very early childhood till the time of our death, we are chasing time. We are always in a hurry. We look at time delays in the same way as we see pain and suffering. If I were to get some job done, I will feel very uncomfortable if it gets delayed. If I were to reach somewhere, I would be continuously worrying about the time it takes to reach the destination. While we are busy in chasing something, we miss something important. We fail to perceive!

We depend on (the concept of) time to understand and perceive reality. Observing through time allows us to see everything in terms of a story, something that has a beginning, a sequence of events, and some end. We have habituated in immersing ourselves in all sort of stories. Anything that does not have a story, has no meaning for us. In fact, we depend upon stories (and therefore, time) so much that many times when there is no sequencing of events, we invent them. One easiest example to understand this is Political Elections.

Election results are just like any other exam results. Someone gets the highest votes and wins. In exams too, candidates answer the questions and are graded and ranked. Yet, the election results are not disclosed at the very end like any other exam. They are disclosed while they are still being counted. This creates an artificial sequence of events as if the candidates are running against each other like in a race. Revealing poll results on real-time basis as they are counted creates artificial excitement, anxiety and emotions whereas in reality, the results are already locked and there is no real racing among the candidates.

Our infatuation with *time* is to such a great degree that it affects everything that gets done in this world. If we look at the world around us, we see most people suffering incompleteness in life. There are those who are overweight and wish to lose weight, and some who are short and want to gain height. Some desire more money and other want better health. Yet, their real worry is not about losing the weight, gaining height or making more money as much as it is about how fast this can be achieved. It is this impatience of the masses that makes them susceptible to different forms of deceptions because they lose their grip on perception. A few smart ones know how to grab this opportunity and take advantage of people's vulnerability where they are in so much hurry that they do not perceive things as they should. The market is full of products that claim to satisfy your endless desires to become slimmer, fairer, smarter, or healthier in quickest possible time. They come up with claims to make you lose tens of pounds of weight in a matter of a week or two. In our desires to get our desires fulfilled as quickly as possible, we continue to chase them endlessly all our lives and yet cannot ever become aware of such a deception.

There is no end to what one can desire in this world. While most humanity might be fighting for their basic necessities such as food and shelter, some of the lucky ones are not just satisfied with a nice car to drive. Instead, they would want to see their car speeding past most other vehicles on the road. In a quest to become fastest and quickest they lose the opportunity to enjoy all that is available to them in the present moment. This kind of behavior also gives an opportunity to a few car makers who know how to attract their buyers with the claims that their cars can accelerate from 0 to 60 miles in a matter of few seconds. It is not clear how a person who can waste hours everyday watching television, discussing irrelevant issues and indulging in useless activities, suddenly desires to save a few seconds when it comes to driving a car!

Everyone needs a permanent place for shelter. This is a basic need of all life. We all aspire to find comfort in our own homes. When we cannot afford to buy a house, we borrow money on loan from some financial institutions. The time of repayment for such loans is a long time; somewhere in the range of ten to thirty years. In a way, it is like spending your whole life trying to replay your borrowed money. Nobody is comfortable with being stuck with anything lasting over a long period of time. When we are tied-in to a loan and are paying off the money slowly over time, we wish to get it repaid as soon as possible. This leads to many more businesses out there who would claim to come to our rescue with ideas about how to pay off our debts quickly. We will never be free (of our worries) as long as we look forward to something, especially when we look forward to doing it faster. *If we are not free, we are not going to achieve total perception ever.*

We are in a hurry all the time. We are in a hurry to start something quickly and then, when it has started, we are in a hurry to finish it off quickly. If you are in a school, you look forward to going to college soon. Once in college, you are eager to finish it and start some job or a business. When in a job, you are always eager to get ahead of others. You want to get to the top earlier and faster than everybody else. When you have worked for many years earning money and chasing some illusory goal, you look forward to retiring as quickly as possible. Our whole journey of life is a race to reach to the next station. But when we reach a station, we do not stop. We do not stop to breathe, relax, look around and enjoy the destination. Instead, we immediately start running and chasing the next station. Moreover, we do not simply chase a target. We chase it against the *time*. And we continue to run until we are dead.

Mark saw Steve in the corridor just outside the conference room. It was announced that Steve was promoted. Mark congratulated him. Steve replied, "This is unacceptable! I should have been promoted two years back. Now I don't care!"

In our eagerness to go there and get that faster makes us lose sight of everything else. If one achieves it, the satisfaction does not last more than a few days. If one does not achieve it, the frustration lasts lifetime. In any case, one fails to perceive. A perception is not limited to what happens to you. A total perception is about knowing everything that goes around you. If one can feel one's own frustration of not achieving something, one must also feel the excitement of others achieving it. While it is natural to feel bad about not getting something, it must not stop one from appreciating the good that is happening around. In appreciating others' happiness or sympathizing with their pain, one moves closer to perceiving much more clearly, much more thoroughly.

If we are given a problem, we look forward to solving it as soon as we can. If we are unable to come to some solution soon, we drop the problem and move ahead. Only when the problem is extremely important, we do not drop it but continue to work towards its solution. But even in such conditions, we are eager to get to a solution fast. We do not like delays because our eyes are always on (the time it takes to reach) the final destination. With such restlessness, impatience, and a hurry to move past any given moment, there is no chance one could ever perceive in totality.

It is not surprising to find that everyone is chasing time all their lives. We have been trained to do so. We have attributed the idea of IQ and intelligence with time. From the very early times, humans are introduced to testing their mental (or physical) abilities on the basis of their performance against time. If one cannot solve given problems in a given time, one is labelled dumb. If one is being interviewed and given a problem, one is expected to solve it in a matter of a minute or two. The fact is that intelligence has nothing to do with how fast or how soon one can solve a problem. Intelligence means ability to solve a problem or even an ability to *attempt* to solve a problem even if no appropriate solution could ever be achieved. Nevertheless, as long as the society will go on giving importance to fastest, quickest and earliest ones, the humankind will continue to miss its opportunity to perceive anything at all.

A total or complete perception cannot happen (if we exist) in *time*. At the time of total perceiving, there is no memory, no concept of *time* in terms of past experiences, no recognition, or future expectation. At the same time, it is also true that we cannot exist outside *time*. If we are made to exist outside the realm of time, we will be lost and perplexed. A timeless existence is free of concepts because there can be no knowledge about anything except for the moment we are in. These two possibilities are mutually exclusive; while we exist in *time*, a complete perception is possible only out of *time*. This can only mean that a yearning for a total and complete perception becomes nothing more than a wishful thinking for humans.

The idea of *time* begins with recognition. A recognition happens with the use of memory. When our attention catches a pattern that matches with a similar pattern from our memory, we recognize it. This process involves *time* because it needs memory to recognize, and the memory is nothing but *time*; It is something from the past. *Time* is something that does not exist in the present moment. If anything is from a memory of the past or an expectation of tomorrow, it is an entity in *time*. Then, we have another habit that goes with recognition, the habit of naming. When we recognize something, we recognize a name associated with the pattern. If somehow, we fail to remember the name, we are fully convinced that we have not recognized it. We think that we are failing to recognize a thing because we are unable to recall the name associated with it. It is our conditioning that makes us think that a name is needed in our ability to observe. We are so programmed that our act of looking is not simply an act of looking, it is an act of looking 'at something.' If during an observation, we cannot recognize any known form of pattern, we are confused. We do not know what we are trying to look for or look at in such cases. It is simply an impossible task for us to avoid the use of memory, or simply, ignoring names and forms to observe!

Our experiences happen in time. From the moment of recognizing sensations to the time we act and then to the time we observe our actions

We are so programmed that our act of looking is not simply an act of looking, it is an act of looking 'at something.'

and the results of those actions, there exists a long period of time. We tend to pay no attention to this passage of time and instead, observe all our actions, responses and results oblivious of this delay. This results in a broken perception of the reality and our inability to cope with the mistakes that happen. The reality is that there are many things that happen during the passage of time from the initial moment to the later times. During this finite period, the observer becomes more mature, more experienced and gets updated with a huge data of memory from various events that take place. Such an observer is incapable of separating the initial actor who had no such experience and maturity from the final observer who is now mature and experienced. In every act when someone points out a mistake, the observer tries to observe his initial actions from the position of his final level of maturity and tries to justify all his actions and ignore any mistakes. A total perception cannot happen unless one realizes that every passing moment brings countless changes, from the actor to the surroundings to the final observer. Therefore, it is simply not possible to observe any act with complete understanding unless it happens in a single moment, without the passage of (noticeable) time.

Our inability to understand the *time* in the way it progressively changes ourselves as well as everything around us makes us question how we could time travel or change our past. It is one of the favorite questions of all interviewers who ask what someone would do differently if one had to relive one's life. Many interviewers also try to evaluate the candidates' state of mind by asking where they might see themselves five or ten years later. The person investigating such scenario forget that when observation or observed change, the observer changes too. In a hypothetical scenario where you could see yourself in past, you are really not in past, but in a projection of the present and imagining it as a past. In such a situation you are breaking the observer from the observed in the past scenario. You believe that these are separate entities where a new and updated version of the observer can be placed in the original observation. *If I could go back to past*. As if I am separate from the past I lived.

We perceive using our sense organs. We observe too using the sense organs. An observation is nothing but an act of perception. We spend most of our time utilizing the act of seeing for the purpose of observation. Yet, in real sense, any form of perceiving can be called an observation. If one is in a dark room, or if one's eyes are closed, one will attempt to use the sense of hearing and that of touch to ascertain the surroundings. In such situation, one can be said to be observant, even though the eyes are not being utilized for observation. We have been trained for thousands of years to observe using our memory. We utilize our memory to recall the name and form matching current observation. At any single moment, we are not simply observing. Instead, we are continuously recalling images from our memory collection and comparing them with our current observation. We are engaged in *time* all the times.

> **If the memory is used in observation, nothing new or fresh will ever be observed, because all such observations happen in *time*.'**

Observation in *time* also means boredom. Every observable scene or a situation becomes known in a very short time. Once something becomes known, it is not fun to keep observing it anymore. We are always in search of something new because we are bored of everything that is old and already known to us. Yet, when we encounter something new, we fail to observe it with a fresh look. At such times, due to our habits, we again attempt to compare the observed with the known memory of the past. We explored this behavior in first chapter and mentioned that the mind can only notice change. At this juncture, it is worth knowing that our sense organs are nothing but an extension of the mind. There is no real separation between the working of the minds and the sense organs. They work in unison - as a combined whole. Therefore, this endless cycle continues in our lives where the mind tries to look for something fresh, interesting, and worthy and yet it ends up in disappointment due to its limitation in perceiving completely. The perceiving is limited because the mind does not know how to observe without bringing in the memory of the past. If the memory is used in observation, nothing new or fresh will ever be observed, because all such observations happen in (the realm of) *time*.

A total perception is not possible unless we know how to drop *time*. If we can realize that we are running all the time, all we need to do is to come to a stop. If we have a deep-rooted habit of observing through our conditioned thought and memory, all we need to do is to stop trying to relate our past experiences with the current happenings. Our association with names and forms plays a major role in our trying to recognize objects, people, and situations. If we need to get out of the bounds of time and perceive completely, we will need to drop our fascination with names and forms. In other words, a way to total and comprehensive perception will be seen as an utterly impossible thing! It is truly so for humans. Yet, those who would take this challenge, dive into the inner world of human mind, and meditate on the nature of the self and the universe, might have a possibility.

> *A Total Perception only is possible when*
> 1. *We are not eager to reach somewhere.*
> 2. *We are not eager to get something, drop something or finish something.*
> 3. *We do not give too much value to experiences.*
> 4. *We stop trying to 'know.'*
> 5. *We stop taking interest in the story behind real life events.*

Separation

As long as we exist in separation, we cannot experience total perception.

A total or complete perception cannot happen in absence of *love*. At the time of perceiving completely, there is no concept of separation in terms of me, you, this, or that. But at the same time, we humans do not know how to love; we are completely untouched with it. That which we think we know about *love* is nothing but an idea of attachment, along with an element of pleasure in it. This idea of separation is seated deeply in our minds. We exist in this world assuming ourselves as having an independent existence. For each of us this deep sense of separation makes us view our world as having two distinct sides. These two parts are me (or mine) and the others. What we consider as ours includes our parents, our children, our relatives, friends, and the property we own. Anything that we do not relate to or we do not want to possess falls in the second category. When we view the world as having such two distinctions, our sense of perception becomes broken, biased, and distorted.

Our attachments and closeness to things and people is not as simple as it might seem. When we feel something or somebody as very close to us, it is not simply about its physical proximity. We consider something as ours only when we feel that we have full freedom to interact with it or control it. The physical closeness does not make something ours, because if that were the case, we would consider insects, birds or mice as our close ones because they occupy the same house as we do. But they are not, because we do not have any control on them. They are there because we cannot somehow get rid of them. If something cannot be controlled by us, we do not consider it ours. On a different note, we also feel very close to everything that we like, desire, or admire even if it is not in our possession or in our proximity. We try to defend and protect every such thing, as we would defend everything that we already possess. We can be found fighting for the politician we like, the celebrity we admire or the sport team we enjoy watching. In such cases we are neither close to them physically, nor do we possess them or have a power to control them. It is simply that we like them or are in love with them and maybe want to become somewhat like them at some point of time.

Our ideas of what is ours and what is not (ours) can be easily figured out by looking the amount of control we have on them. We might live in a rental house for many years and still not consider or treat it as our own. We damage the walls and doors by pushing countless nails, let our kids write on the walls and let our dogs and cats pee everywhere around the property. Even though we spend years living in the house and continue to use and touch everything in the house, we exist in that surrounding with a strong conviction that those walls, floors, carpets, and the furniture are not ours. On the contrary, a newly purchased house or a car immediately becomes very dearly to us. We immediately become concerned about keeping the car clean and tidy as if it were related to us for many years. We have such strange criteria for feeling affectionate towards objects! This affection of ours is not just limited to lifeless objects. We may stop considering our children as ours if we do not feel we have any control over them. There are many cases where parents send their own kids out of their house, or even disown them. It is not just about the physical objects or the people, but even the ideas that we generate that we give them far more value than the ideas that belong to others. Our endless discussions and conflicts with each other's ideologies has its roots in the same philosophy, "*My idea is better than your idea.*" With such an idea of separation between ourselves and the others, when we view two objects, one of which happens to be ours, our observation ceases to be a realistic view of the world. Our sense of perception becomes far from being comprehensive, total, or absolute. We instantly develop a bias splitting the world into two parts creating a unique version of the world around us – our 'personal universe'. Having created our personal universe with such broken perception, we humans have made our universe a home ground of conflicts, bondage, and suffering.

From the description so far, it seems that we all have been behaving like this since forever. However, this is not the case. We all were born with an ability to perceive the world as it existed, defined, and understood through the limitations of our sense organs. As children, we all are born with an unbiased point of view because we do not have any idea about what is ours and what is not. As children, we just go about anywhere, pick anything from anywhere, and talk to anyone without reservations. We look at the world as it is; playful! Our view of the world as a child remains pure and unadulterated. Thereafter, we soon grow up to establish a personalized version of this universe with our own stock of likes, dislikes, jealousy, greed, and desires for unlimited possessions.

This idea of separation in human minds has led Psychologists to identify different types of biases in us. When we look at the world with a divided perspective, we tend to give different weightage to things depending on who owns them. We give more value to things that we possess or the work that we do compared to others' possession or actions. We get a great satisfaction when we are working for ourselves or for the ones whom we consider ours. Psychologists call such a bias as Endowment bias where people tend to give more value to things just because they own them. Imagine the case where in a competition, one of the candidate's mother happens to be in the jury. It is doubtful if her evaluation of the son or daughter will not be affected by her strong attachment to him or her. We all can visualize a scenario where a teacher of a class also happens to be the father of one of the students. These are real possibilities and many such cases do exist in our daily lives. Those teachers and judges cannot escape the endowment bias. People cannot simply get away from this innate bias. When a group dance is performed on a stage, every parent whose child is a part of the group performance, is only interested in how his or her child is performing. They never observe the group performance at all. They only observe their child in the large crowd. It is only when someone does not know any individual participant in a group, can he or she observe the group dance, without any special interest in a particular participant. *One can only observe completely when one is a total stranger, knowing nobody, remembering nobody, and expecting nothing.*

Our attachment to certain things or ideas or aversion from them affects our perception of facts and thereby our ability to make appropriate decisions. Our legal institutions and the judiciary are aware of this common flaw in our behaviors. Therefore, there is a selection criterion in place when a few people are randomly summoned for a jury duty appearance. Before shortlisting the members of a jury, the judge asks some questions to each of them to ascertain if they have any biases related to the issue of crime. I was told once a person was once summoned for a jury duty related to a case of car accident involving drunk driving. The judge had asked each of the prospective members of jury if they had any religious or cultural reservations about use of alcohol. This person told her that his religion as well as his family values did not think very highly of those who consumed alcohol. The judge then spared him from being a part of the jury because she was aware that his judgment about the case might be influenced by his negative view of alcoholics. A total perception is a distant possibility as long as we are not able to overcome our petty little division of the world of *me and my precious opinions* versus, *they and their petty opinions.*

This sense of separation due to a bias between what is ours and what is not ours is more detrimental when more people work together. When they work together in a group, each one tends to give more weightage to his or her own contribution. Whereas we imagine that when two people come to work together, or when two big corporations are made to merge their businesses, they both might achieve more than what they could achieve by operating independently. In reality, this scenario becomes more idealistic than a reality because for achieving a synergy between two or more entities, a harmony needs to exist. Our inherent tendency to divide the world into two parts, *mine* and *not mine* makes it difficult to imagine two different people or two big corporations to be able to work in harmony. When each person wants to allocate more weightage to one's own contribution, whether it is about the opinions or efforts, a state of harmony between different individuals is unimaginable.

Achieving harmony between different people, groups or nations is only possible when their perceptions are free of bias and conflict, a total perception! The reality is, however, quite the opposite! It is the major reason why all humanity is divided. The only way this bias could be removed is by removing the idea of *me* and *mine* from our minds. It is when this idea of I is gone, the imaginary separation in the human mind gets dropped too. You need two to create a separation; when one is gone, the other goes too, and so does the division or separation between the two. *Love* is nothing but the dropping of 'I' from one's consciousness. When one drops one's sense of 'I', the sense of individuality, then all the divisions get dropped, and the whole world becomes a unified experience. This experience is nothing but *love*, which we are far from experiencing with our current limitations. In our fear to let go our little self, we miss the opportunity to become the larger self, the all-inclusive persona which experiences the world completely, without the pain, suffering conflicts or fears. You might say, a total perception is nothing but an experience of pure Love.

There are more ways we continue to discriminate between the things looking from a biased perspective. Our discriminatory approach in viewing things based on our possession of them also creates a psychological conflict within ourselves. In a realistic world, one would imagine that the pain of losing an object would equate to the value associated with its acquisition. On the contrary, it is seen that once we acquire something, our pain of losing it becomes much more because of our disproportionate valuation of the things that we own.

One can easily relate that the pain of losing a ten-dollar bill is far more than the pleasure of finding a ten-dollar bill in a street. This pattern of *loss aversion* is one of the biases that translates the real world into the world of conflicts for us. We do not feel the pain of others in the same way as we feel our own pain. Quite simply, we approach differently in perceiving pain as it happens to us versus it happening to others. It should not be surprising to come to know that the ideas of pains and pleasures are born out of our own mind, due to the imperfect way we perceive the world around us.

The ideas of pains and pleasures are born out of our own minds, due to the way we perceive the world around us.

Most people do understand pain and suffering that goes around us. However, those are not perceived as comprehensively as they should be. Instead, they are seen partially, incompletely and in a biased way. In another behavioral pattern, people are seen not paying equal attention to everything that happens around them. They tend to pay more attention to immediate and relatable things in front of them. They generally tend to feel more sympathetic towards specific type of a victim in comparison to a large vaguely defined group with the similar needs. This type of bias in people's perception is known as the *identified victim effect* whereby they are more inclined to help identified individual victim compared to a group of people with the same need. Many organizations tend to exploit this unique inclination of ours towards identifiable objects and people through their campaigns and advertisements. When the different charities run their campaigns, they introduce real looking faces and names in their campaigns and messages. This makes their campaign more relatable and allow people to come forward easily to help 'those' people. The picture is very clear. If you won't perceive the world totally as you must, there are others who would make you perceive it as they want you to perceive according to their (planted) ideas.

There is another known human behavior known as *effort justification*, where people tend to show asymmetry in comparing two outcomes. They are commonly seen to

Efforts put in some actions make a great difference in the way the outcomes are perceived.

attribute a higher value to the outcome of some task that they have put efforts into. People can be seen cherishing their first earned salary or being attached to an ugly looking piece of object that they built themselves. One of my neighbors spends a good amount of time in his backyard working in his kitchen garden. He grows many different vegetables and fruits there. Many times, when I visit him, he proudly displays the pomegranates and tomatoes that grew in his yard which are odd shaped, quite small, and very sour. Yet, he enjoys everything that he grows and relishes eating them. Since he has put efforts into growing them himself, he looks at his produce very differently than anyone else. There is nothing wrong in enjoying the things as they are, but it is quite certain that the same person would have avoided the same ugly looking or sour fruits when available in the market.

When it comes to success, people can be seen to attribute their own skills, efforts, and qualities responsible for their success. Talk to any millionaire how he got rich and he would be able to show hundreds of good things that he did that made him successful. Most of the actions that they would mention are the same as anyone else does or can do. Yet, the successful individuals sincerely believe that it was their habit of reading books, or their hard-work or their discipline about something that made them rich. This same *self-serving bias* also makes them blame all their failures to the forces outside their control.

One of the downfalls of such an attitude of separation is that people cannot understand issues, problems or difficulties faced by those whom they do not consider related to them. It is understandable in cases where people did not themselves have any experience with those kinds of problems. For example, if I never experienced physical pain in my life, I would not understand the pain faced by others when I see them falling hard on floor. Quite surprisingly, people continue to carry the same attitude of indifference towards others in all those areas which they would not ignore for themselves. Everyone knows the pain of hunger and poverty. Yet, the sight of extreme poverty in the third word does not seem to affect most people. Those same people might not be able to withstand the pain of coming to know that their children missed their morning breakfast! This differential feeling due to the idea of separation in human beings is an example of incomplete perception. With such imperfect ways of perceiving our surroundings, we miss experiencing our magical cosmos showering its radiance all around.

It is for such reasons that a total and complete perception remains a far-off target to achieve for most humans. They behave differently for success and failures in the same way they experience the gains and losses differently. It is always about oneself versus the others and it works in the same manner whether it is about possessions, opinions, efforts, or relationships. If something goes bad, it is always someone else's fault. Yet, when things are going well, outside factors do not seem to create much concern.

There is yet another way people skew their sense of perception when they evaluate themselves against others. People tend to display an illusory superiority in the sense that they overestimate their own qualities and abilities in relation to the same qualities and abilities in others. When people look at the same task done by themselves as well as others, they rate their own efforts as superior compared to the others.

At many other times, when observing others, people tend to make *fundamental attribution error* which is sometimes also known as *correspondence bias*. They tend to believe that what people do reflects what they are. In other words, people's interpretation of their own behavior is different than their understanding of similar behavior from others. In explaining the behavior of other people, they tend to put undue emphasis on their internal characteristics rather than the external factors. This is a commonly seen behavior. When we see a person driving very fast on a road, we are inclined to assume that it is a rash driver, or that the person driving the car is insensitive about others on the road. We would never give a thought that he or she might be in some danger or an emergency. Such tendency is also seen in situations where we easily blame all external factors to our own failures such as insufficient light, or broken pencil or delayed train, but immediately label others as lazy, insincere or irresponsible if they happen to be late in the same or similar situations.

Our perceptions are also skewed depending on our skills, expertise, and experiences. This biased estimation affects people's understanding and evaluation of someone's job. It so happens that people with lower skills usually overestimate their capabilities whereas highly skilled people tend to underestimate their capabilities. This kind of behavior is known as *Dunning-Kruger effect."*

There are a couple of hundred such ways as mentioned here where a perceived separation between individuals make them look at an unbroken reality and break it up by creating a bias between what they think is theirs and that which they think is not theirs. Those who are interested in psychology can find more details about such biases as researched by the scientists. As long as such illusory separation will remain in the minds of individuals, they will never be able to see things the way they are. The nature of this bias is such that even those who will make conscious efforts to get past them might not succeed. The idea of separation lies deep in the consciousness of human beings and is a slow and steady accumulation due to thousands of years of conditioning.

A Total Perception only is possible when
1. *We do not have a strong sense of identification.*
2. *We feel pain for every living creature.*
3. *We love everything in this universe in the same way.*

Logical Reasoning

Logic and reasoning shut the doors of Perception

Logics and reasonings are the pillars of our modern knowledge. We invest all our knowledge and intellect in studying, analyzing, and interpreting various behaviors and processes through logic and reasoning. Science and scientific studies rely on this approach and the use of logic and reasoning has become an accepted means of accepting or rejecting any idea, theory, or a proposal. Our heavy dependence on logical reasoning makes us to ignore some very fundamental mistakes in the process of decision making which leads us to make strange choices.

> *Every morning I weigh myself. The machine shows 68 Kg. Then I wear my glasses. The machine now shows 88 Kg. My glasses must weigh 20 Kg.*

A logic has two opposite states, such as *yes* and *no* or *true* and *false* or *good* and *bad*. Each one is an exact opposite of other. According to the reasoning based on logics, if two entities are equal, then opposite of one is also equal to the opposite of the other. Going by this reasoning, it would be fair to assume that if one idea or one action is good, then its opposite would be bad. In most of the situations, our use of logic seems to work reasonably well; For example, if people are told that smoking is injurious to health, then they get the message that not smoking must be not bad for health which is same as being good for health.

The nature of communication among humans is very complex. We not only come from very different cultural, historical, or political backgrounds, but we also communicate in different languages. Yet, the major difficulty in being able to perceive and understand each other is not due to our cultural or linguistic difference but due to our limited understanding of emotions. The logical reasoning works only on two distinctly opposite states, yet we use it on countless state of emotions. When someone fails in love, he or she immediately embraces hatred. It seems reasonable because love and hate seem to be exactly opposite states. This mistaken approach is a result of ignoring the fact that there are not just two emotions, but thousands of different emotions between any two humans. As a rightful approach toward using logic correctly, the opposite of love must be to 'not love'. If one has failed in love, one should have changed one's approach not to love the other person anymore. The approach of using hatred as the opposite of love is flawed, because when you hate, you are still related to the person with the same intensity as you were with love. By choosing to hate instead of simply not loving, you have not let the person get away from your memories. Whereas, as a correct approach, if you do not love anymore, you completely break all the bonds and therefore become free of all emotions including hate towards the other person.

Even if we stick to two exact opposite states (duality) as our (only) means of survival in this world of infinite possibilities, a logical deduction might miss the Truth. Can you imagine a situation when someone says, "I always lie?" This is an impossible situation and a completely illogical one. If the person always lies, in this particular statement the person is not lying. If the person does not always lie, then too this statement becomes false. What if someone says, "I am humble!" This is a perfectly logical statement yet is never true in reality. A tall person can say I am tall and be truly a tall person, but a humble person cannot claim to be humble and be humble at the same time. It is clear that a logic that works well in one situation fails to be true in another. This itself means that a logical reasoning does not ensure truth in all conditions or at all places. Reality is a complex combination of countless possibilities. Trying to explain and understand it with only two opposite poles of logical reasoning is a very crude approximation.

The problematic approach of using logic blindly without being mindful of our actions is evident is many situations. In societies where the superior class oppressed inferior classes for many centuries or where men displayed cruel behavior against women, the rationalists find it perfectly justifiable if its opposite is made to happen. The only reason most people find it justified now for the oppressed class to take revenge against the superior classes or for the women to display cruel behavior against men is that if the previous act was bad, then its opposite must be good. If they would have understood that the opposite of oppression is 'not-oppression', they would have seen that by favoring women's oppression towards men, they have repeated the same mistake which they thought were correcting by choosing the exact opposite. In true sense, a situation of oppression can only be countered by ensuring no oppression by anybody over anyone.

In a similar situation, many studies believed that in American workplaces, there was no 'balanced' representation of different races of people. For some unique reasons, they must have thought of some reasonable numbers of representation of different races which might appear to them as the 'right' kind of diversity. The simple (flawed) reasoning would say that if something is not balanced or diverse, then opposite of that must be balanced or diverse. They figured out that in workplaces, Asian women seemed to be very low in numbers. The only rational or logical solution that seemed reasonable to them was that an attempt to increase Asian females in the workplace must be a valid display of implementing 'diversity'. As a result, all around the world, companies, governments, and different groups have been practicing such discriminatory practices of choosing one (group) over other (group) to implement non-discrimination.

In another example of limitation of logic and reason, in some situations when a general statement is made, a restriction is assumed without being specified. When I ask someone to name a month that contains 29 days, listeners assume that the month should contain only 29 days. The idea that every single month contains 29 days (or more) does not occur to the logical working mind. This is a very common tendency of human mind which is exploited the most everyday. When you see a photo or a video clip of a person drinking alcohol, you assume that the person drinking alcohol is the only truth which leads you to believe that he might be a regular drinker. When you are given some little example of someone's lie, you label the person as a liar and believe this to be true at all times. In political elections, one small piece of evidence (whether true or imaginary) leads to the defeat of a person because people imagine the evidence to be the whole truth about the person.

A mind could be open to total perception only if it could drop its dependence on (faulty) logical reasonings.

In another situation when a general statement is made, an opposite is assumed without being specified. Let us assume a situation where the Boss asks an employee if his colleague (named Tom) has come to the office. The employee may say that he knows that Tom has come to the office because he has seen him somewhere in the building. A logician might be inclined to assume that if this is a true statement, then its opposite must be false. But such reasoning falls apart because if someone has not seen Tom in the office, it might not necessarily mean that he has not come to the office. It does not change anything even if every single person in the office says that they have not seen Tom in the office that day. Nothing will ever prove if Tom is not in the office. Only Tom's presence can be proved, not his absence!

There is a slightly different variation where people use rational logic using one scenario to explain a contrasting situation with use of opposites. My brother has two daughters. It happens many times that when he makes a statement about one of his daughters, his other daughter misinterprets it by applying rationality. Once he said that his elder daughter was very good at handling difficult situations, the younger one felt offended and immediately responded with a counter as if he had meant that the younger one was not good at handling difficult situations. The logical mind assumes the two daughters as two poles and uses the rationale that if one is labelled as good then it must mean that the other must be the other pole, the opposite of good.

In one of the most common ways people use rationalization is by bringing in another data like the one in picture. When someone is pointed a mistake or a peculiar behavior, one misses the opportunity of a total perception because of one's strong need to rationalize. In a recent development in the country when the Narcotics department was questioning Deepika about her alleged drug related chat, one of her followers was seen asking on a television debate why another film star Kangana was not being questioned. This is the most common defense seen in use by everybody. Even in a primary class, when a kid is asked why he did not complete his homework, his favorite response is that others also didn't do it. It is always easy to shift a blame to others and when it seems logical, then there is no better way to get a quick relief. A mind cannot stand being pointed out, being blamed, being questioned, or being made responsible for something bad. This logical approach of presenting a parallel example comes to their rescue.

The logical field is only made of two contrasting states. It has no place for any other information besides these opposite poles. This leads people to oversimplify any real-life situation and fill all the unknown grey areas with one of the two alternatives available in any situation. When I ask someone to name someone who tells truth, it is assumed that the person must only tell the truth and not the lies (at some other time). Even if someone would come up with a name of such a person who have almost always told truth, there is a possibility of someone else disagreeing because of one strange case of his or her lie. A logical mind will not settle for any state other than a complete black and a complete white. No amount of grey is agreeable to it. To allow for the mind to overcome such rigid logical and rational boundary, one must specifically mention about the grey areas or probable zones in the alternatives.

Tom was driving in the mountains when he came across a dangerous turn. He was surprised that there was no warning sign to alert him. He asked his friend who had been visiting this area for a long time. His friend said that they had a warning sign there for three years. They recently removed it because it seemed useless to put a warning board when there were no accidents happening.

These kinds of logical explanations are very common among people. Currently the whole world has been fighting a pandemic. Different health and government organizations have been urging people to wear mask while in public areas. Absence of any treatment and non-availability of vaccines have made it one of the worst diseases in human history. Some countries enforced a voluntary shutdown while others continue to operate but with strict rules about wearing masks. Those who have been wearing the mask all the time when in public and finding it inconvenient have already started skipping it. They are slowly becoming more casual about safe social-distancing or wearing face masks. Their logic is that if nothing has happened to them in such a long time, why wear masks!

The use of logic seriously affects our sense of judgment about people, things, and processes. Let's picture who is an introvert and does not feel comfortable coming out in front of a crowd performing or presenting. If someone is enjoying dancing on the stage and calls this to join in the fun and dance, he might say that he does not like the idea of presenting himself in front of a large audience. The other person (rational mind) is most likely to interpret his statement as if he is trying to mean that it is not a good idea for *anyone* to dance and behave like that in public. The logic has a limited domain. My idea of dancing in public cannot be equated with another person's dancing because I could an introvert while the other might not be. What is not good for me might be perfectly alright for the other because what seems good for an extrovert might not be the same for an introvert. However, the logic or rational interpretation does not care about the totality of an information. It only knows how to slice every piece of data into two states and then make an intelligent looking decision based on the incomplete information in that data. A total perception cannot happen as long as we have a strong need of using the reasoning based on such faulty logic.

Reality does not care about logic. Sometimes a completely irrational statement might be perfectly right. When one says that an intelligent person is one who knows of his or her stupidities, you can read the underlying message. On the face, this looks counter-intuitive. In the language of logic, it is very similar to a statement which says that if it knows that it is not A, then it is A. If a person is intelligent, how could he or she be stupid? It seems illogical but it is not. It is one of those profound truths that many seem to ignore. The reality is that intelligent people can only be those who know about their weaknesses and mistakes. Otherwise, if they were not aware of their mistakes, how would they overcome them? If they could not overcome them, how could they be called intelligent?

One who knows this paradox, comes to know the secret of almost anything. Then one never looks at the idea of peace with an ignorant mind trying to be quiet or searching for a silence in its surrounding. One who is accustomed of such paradox, knows that peace is achieved when one knows about one's restlessness or absence of peace. In the same way, one does not tirelessly search for an illusory harmony when one clearly comes to understand that a harmony is nothing but an awareness of one's disharmony, or that a mindfulness is becoming aware of one's absent-mindedness. In short, knowing absence of something is to know the thing.

> *There were a lot of weeds in my backyard. Having been overlooked for a couple of weeks, they had grown their roots strongly in the ground. I do not prefer to use any herbicide to kill the weeds but instead pull them out by hands. One day I decided to do something about it so went out and started watering them with a hose. My daughter saw me and wondered why I was watering the weeds, because it only means that I wanted them to grow more. This was a perfectly logical interpretation from her end. You water the plants to help them grow. Logically there could be no other meaning to watering the weeds. The logic would not know on the fact of the situation that the water loosens the clay and makes it easy to pull them out along with their roots.*

There is another behavior which is completely illogical but makes absolute sense in everyday life. One would normally assume that it is illogical to observe a completely opposite behavior when some action is performed with an intention of an expected behavior. For example, when you add fertilizer to a growing plant, a growth or an increase in its height is expected. If adding fertilizer to the plant results in shrinking the plant, you would call it illogical. In real life, many such actions exist which defy logic. One such behavior is humility. Humility is something that is missing in anybody who wants to be humble. It can only be there when one does not try to be so. One can attempt to be humble by imitating some actions or modifying the voice tone or speaking and behaving in friendly manner, but all such actions are superficial and easily noticed by others as fake.

There is another way we use logic in our daily lives. It is about finding cause and action relation between any two sequential events. For anything to happen, we must find a reason to exist prior to the event. We are restless unless we find out cause for anything to happen. We call it science. We call it logical to relate two events where one seems to have caused the other. If there is smoke, we find it logical to have a fire somewhere. Use of such a logic is practical and comes handy in living our live smartly and wisely. Yet, trying to find a reason for everything makes us miss the beauty, mystery and vastness of the universe around us. In our quest to find answers to everything, we forget to notice anything. If it is raining, we must find out why it is raining at this time rather than simply watching the rain or getting immersed in experiencing it completely.

Our understanding of logical reasonings extend into the realm of morality, righteousness, and justice too. We all have been brought up with the ideas of rights and wrongs based on our religion, our culture and our social norms. We are able to use a variety of logical techniques and causation into forming our own views of what should happen in all areas which agrees our version of the truth. We even question Gods if we see that there is no logical explanation (causation relation) for someone getting punished even after doing so much good in the life. We question why small innocent kids die from cancer and why corrupts and criminals enjoy all the comforts in life. We question why it doesn't rain when it should and why people die in millions from diseases. Our idea of logic is based on our version of life around us. We believe that there are somethings good and other things bad. If one does good, then it is logical that everything good happens to him or her. Our idea of good means that one should not suffer, one should not die before getting too old.

Logic and reasoning are a great way to understand and solve many issues. Many scientific experiments make use of rationality, logic and decision making to discover new theories and concepts. We need to understand that the use of logic works only two distinctly separate halves. When we use such reasonings on continuous reality, we risk losing all the shades of such reality and perceive only the black and white out of countless shades of greys in between. A total perception is not possible with an unaware use of rational logic in real situations. On the contrary, trying to absorb the reality without being attached to logic has better prospects for a total perception.

A Total Perception only is possible when
  1. *We stop looking and interpreting life with rational mind.*

Denying Reality

When we look, we always look for what must be, not what is.

Our existence is real, yet we seem to live an illusory life. We do not perceive the world as it is. We only perceive it the way we wish it must be. At every moment, the life is happening; it is changing, transforming, dying as well as being born afresh. Yet, we are stuck in a dream-like world of our own. We do not seem to notice anything around us. We do not notice that everything is changing shape, color, size, quality, and behavior. Or maybe, we notice all changes but take them for granted. We assume everything is completely structured, predictable, bound, controlled and secure. Quite paradoxically, we even assume all change to be predictable. We believe in certainty, permanence, constancy, repeatability and above all a complete security. Security is only in something *known*. To be unknown, uncertain, and impermanent means insecurity. Humans are afraid of uncertainty because it means death. It has been this deep-rooted fear of unknown in humans that transformed their way of perceiving reality into imagining an illusory world of permanency and regularity.

All our conflicts have their roots in this behavior of ours; our imagining a different reality than the one out there. For example, we do not like our politicians because we wish they had high moral values. We cannot simply acknowledge a leader with low moral values! The leader might be doing great in all areas of development, safety, jobs, and international relations. Yet, we cannot get away from an image of an ideal leader in our minds which imagines that the leader should not be immoral or untruthful. At those times we forget that morality has nothing to do with leading a country. It is simply our way of denying a reality whenever it is not in agreement with our values, beliefs, or expectations. We also imagine that the leader should have the same opinions that we believe in. If our leaders continue to make decisions that we believe are right, we continue to support them. The moment we see that their opinions are different than ours, we disown them. We cannot simply stay with situations which we do not agree with. We come up with every possible way to deny the existence of facts. By denying reality and creating a shield of alternate facts around us, we find ourselves safe and secure in our illusory shelter.

Michael was diagnosed with high blood pressure long time back. It has been many years since he had been taking pills to control his blood pressure and cholesterol. Whenever someone discussed health issues, he proudly mentioned that his cholesterol and blood pressure were normal, and he was in good health. It made me think and question if that was really the case! How could I call myself normal if I had to take pills to make myself normal? The reality was that his health was not normal. Yet, he chose to ignore the facts; the reality of him not being in good health. Denying reality is very comforting. When you ignore what is happening, you are relieved from taking any action about it. Taking action about something that hurts you needs time, effort and energy. Ignoring that which hurts makes you become free of all the hassle. Therefore, denying a reality which hurts you is the easiest way of putting the burden off your mind.

My neighbor's teenaged daughter started writing in publications as an intern. One day I saw an article that she wrote. I found that the article was full of prejudices, misconceptions, and one-sided opinions. It was obvious that she was influenced by those writers and journalists who had their ill-motived intentions to spread their peculiar ideology among masses. Being concerned about the bias in her perceptions at such young age, I thought of letting her parents know so that they could guide her with right way of approaching journalism and looking at the facts as they must be. When I brought this up with her mother, I was surprised to find that she was not ready to accept that her daughter would have written anything bad. When I showed her this one article which was full of prejudices and biases, she wrote me back pointing to all the other articles that she had written, mentioning that they all were very good. The reality was hurting and the only way not to get hurt was to divert the attention to that which is soothing. She was not talking about the one problem that I was discussing, but instead, was trying to show everything else where there was no problem. When I pursued more and tried to bring her back to this one objectionable article, she denied that the article had any one-sided opinion. She did not find any problem with the article! She added that her daughter was quite young, and she could write anything she wanted to write. I quit. You can talk to someone only when the person is perceiving facts. When someone has already denied the present moment and have drifted away to a safe zone, you have lost the communication.

The reality is that everything that is born will die one day. This death will not come in an instant, but will be a slow process, unless there is an accident. The slow process of aging is a fact which cannot be denied.

> **"The reality was hurting and the only way not to get hurt was to pay attention to that which is soothing."**

It is ugly, painful and has no hope of recovering. At the end of the process of aging is the reality of death. Each one of us is fully aware of this fact. Yet, we spend most of our life in denying this reality and try to make this process to come to a halt or at least slow-down. We are comforted in the idea of an even slower aging which would give us few more years before dying. Many even go further and ponder over some ideas about reversing the process of aging. This denial is prominently seen in every action that we take. As people start aging, their hair starts turning grey. The idea of hair turning grey is not a comforting one; people would do anything to make them look the way they had been. They try to alter the reality and want to continue with our idea of permanence, constancy, and predictability. This leads to our attempting to bring their previous color back through artificial means. We cannot accept our changing body shape, facial hairs, thin lips, unshapely eyebrows, falling hair, aging lines on our face, wrinkles around our eyes and hundreds of such changes that our bodies go through. Therefore, we continue to invest a great amount of money and time on trying to make them look the same way as they used to look. When we deny the reality, we fail to perceive the reality, as it is.

Aging has its own issues besides the body getting weaker, sicker, and breaking apart. When a person gets old, his or her relations get affected. Most people who once found great pride in meeting you, are afraid to meet you and face you anymore. You turn up being more of a liability than being an asset. At one time you might have had a great influence to help others. Now the time is reversed; it is you who would need various types of help such as medical, financial, physical or at the least emotional. You notice your close ones, your friends and your own family members trying to avoid you as much as they can. This is the fact. This is the reality. But this is what we go on denying. We do not miss any opportunity to fight with those who ignore us. We want the old times back. Those times have gone! They are not going to come back! You have become useless to everybody! This is the only fact one needs to acknowledge. You are not important anymore (to all those who are trying to avoid you). There is no way you can win them back to loving you, respecting you or caring for you. If you have seen the life, this is how it goes. You might have seen the same happening with countless old men and women in your own life. Maybe you were not perceiving the truth at that time too, like you are not getting it right now. But we go on denying the reality. We go on giving ourselves far more importance and desire to win our relatives and friends back. We continue to long for the happy days to return rather than accepting the harsh reality of the old age and the times it shows to us. If we learned to accept reality, we would always be content, quiet, and satisfied with what is available to us at any moment.

We are humans and there are always lots of opportunities for things to go wrong. But we are also humans who are programmed not to see ourselves inferior in comparison to others when it comes to our abilities. For this reason, we tend to avoid every scenario where our mistakes can be noticed.

Ordinarily we do not have a real urge to look around at people and notice their mistakes and try to teach them how not to do such mistakes. However, when you are a parent and notice your own child doing something wrong, you feel a responsibility to make the child aware of it and try to make them learn ways not to repeat them in future. You do so for the sole purpose of making them become self-sufficient in taking care of themselves independently. An intelligent person is one who knows his weaknesses. By helping them identifying their mistakes, we want to help them become wiser.

In my own case as a parent, I faced resistance from my child every time I tried to point her mistake. My child would never accept that there was any mistake. She was always ready with some explanation, some reason, or some strange diversion away from the conflicting situation. She denied the facts blatantly. At one time she was at a school function at night and I had a hard time trying to find her among a large group of students. When I tried to talk about the situation later so that she could understand what problem we faced and how we could avoid repeating it in the future, I was surprised that she did not want to talk about it at all! It was so obvious to see that she had no better choice anyways. Either she accepted that there was a mistake, or simply chose to avoid the situation so as not to feel the pain. I could see this dilemma of human mind every time a conflict happened where she did not want me to discuss what had happened. Facing the reality was the biggest nightmare for her. For facing it would show the ugly face of the reality, the reality where some mistakes had happened, and she might have been a prime reason for committing the mistakes. It has been years now, and I still struggle with such situations with her every time a conflict happens.

This world is diverse, dynamic, and chaotic. The reality of this universe is unbroken, continuous, and absolute. We have our own limitations in perceiving the nature of reality in its original form. We cannot understand and apprehend something that goes on forever and ever, so we invented a concept of time. We divided the continuous reality in equal sections of time, invented clock and calendar and tried to make sense of ever-present reality through imaginary realms called the past and the future. We enforced our concepts of regularity, rules, and morality on this universe. We stuck to such artificially created version of reality that has gone far from being real anymore. At present times, we have created a world where our behaviors or gestures are not a true reflection of our natural perception but a conditioned and trained reflection of our social and moral values.

In every section of our society people must be constantly cautious in their actions so that their intentions are not misjudged to be racially biased, discriminatory, or based on prejudices. To safeguard themselves, people must always be on their expected behavior and habitually review their actions and modify them to suit the cultural fit of the society. In India, it is considered disrespectful to touch something or someone with foot. People born and raised there have been trained not to use legs to point toward something or touch anything with their feet. Many actions that you would find easier doing with your feet have to be restrained because of the cultural restrictions. It might be easier to use your foot to push the drawer or pick something from floor without bending or hurting your back, but you would force yourself to avoid doing it in public because it might seem awkward. In the same way, it might be your natural tendency to show anger or fight with someone who is in conflict with you. You might be comfortably in your worst moods when in your home and with your family, yet, in public places, you would avoid conflicts or being rude, harsh, or argumentative with anybody, especially someone who is of a particular color, race or religion because you would not want to avoid being labelled and seen as a racist. Years of our training to adjust to our social and cultural setup makes us behave forcefully, habitually, and conditionally. Living such, we not only do not perceive our surroundings as we should, but we also do not act normally and completely according to our natural instincts based on our perceptions.

It is not only our actions and behavior in public that we need to be constantly vigilant about. It is also the use of words in our language that we need to use with great caution. We do not hesitate to label those who look at reality as it is. If someone sees a black and a white and says so, he is labeled as a racist. If in a competition no female can get through, the competition and its organizers are blamed for being discriminatory. We have not only got into habit of denying reality and creating a 'politically correct' version of universe around us, but we have also ensured that no one can easily perceive the world as it is in its original form. We have made it a crime to observe the reality without artificially toning it down through language, gestures, eulogies, and cover-ups.

This is an unpredictable world, where individual safety is always desired but never achieved completely. The world is a big food chain where stronger ones or intelligent ones are designed to consume weaker or stupid ones. Every creature is on its guards and is cautious of hidden dangers. Now that we have grown a lot in technology and made our lives safe and comfortable, we have started envisioning a fanciful and imaginary world. We have come up with some wonderful ideas of equality, rights, discrimination, socialism, and feminism. In our quest to uphold these concepts of idealism at any cost, we go on denying the reality around us. When people talk about women equality, they seem to ignore everything that might be true but does not support their claim. In reality, a woman roaming alone at night in public area is unsafe. We might have established many laws that commands people not to mistreat or abuse others, but the human laws are not above the laws of the nature. If you have a choice of taking a safe road against an unsafe jungle, and you choose the path of the jungle, you would be a fool to expect the same level of safety and security from the government. In the same way, choosing to roam in the night by choice and expecting the laws or your rights to protect you is a big mistake. An oncoming danger cannot be avoided by shutting your eyes. Accepting the risks in some situations and acting such that ensures you safest alternative is the right way of living. Assuming every situation to be of equal opportunity or risk is denying the reality. It is an individual responsibility to be aware of the reality and make conscious and wise decisions to protect itself. By sticking on to our illusory ideal world, we deny the reality, impede our perceptions, and make ourselves unsafe.

A total perception can only happen in the present moment. The reality in its completeness is all there is in the present moment. To perceive completely is to perceive the reality as it is in this moment. If an observer is not ready to acknowledge everything that is made available to the senses and therefore, perceive the moment in its complete fullness, the universe experienced such will be far from its true form. By denying the reality, we fail to experience a total perception

A Total Perception only is possible when
1. *We look at what is and not what must be.*
2. *We do not run away from criticism or exposing our weaknesses.*
3. *We do not just behave as how the society wants us to behave.*
4. *We try to please others.*

6

Misuse of Energy

If all the energy wasted in useless activity was preserved, a Total Perception could be possible.

A total perception requires immense energy. That energy is quite different from the kind of energy we know. It is not the energy of habits, intention, desire, or purpose. It is far beyond all that. We all have this energy available to us but is not easily accessible to us because of our current wasteful ways. We waste too much of our energy into distractions and unnecessary chores. Such habits make it extremely difficult for us to pay attention and notice hundreds of changes happening around us every moment because we have our interests in something else.

"Why would we need a lot of energy?" you might ask. It is a valid question. We are in a habit of carrying multiple tasks at a time and do not find it a big problem (to be able to reasonably pay attention to them). We manage our families, got out to work, find time to fix problems and do many more activities every day without seeing it as a hassle. Finally, when we hear about the idea of a total perception to gain wisdom and intelligence, we add it too to our existing list of tasks and try to adjust the schedules of our routine life by allocating some time to this new activity also. This is where we are wrong!

Our perceptions have always been incomplete. In fact, we cannot easily grasp anything completely even if we tried hard to pay complete attention. The goal (of total perception) is one of the most difficult ones and it would require a whole lot of energy. What is needed to be done if a goal must be achieved at any cost? Imagine you are driving a car uphill and the gas in the tank is not sufficient to make it to the destination. There is no gas-station in the way, and it is not possible to turn back and try to look for a gas station on the way back because it is becoming dark already. What do you do? The gas is limited, and your purpose is simply to reach the destination. You figure out that nothing else matters except for you to be at the destination. Your journey till now was quite comfortable. You have been carrying plenty of food and drinks in the car's trunk. You also have a camping tent and a few chairs packed on the top of the car. You have been enjoying the trip listening to the music and enjoying the cool air from the air-conditioner. Yet, at this moment, nothing matters except for you to reach the top of the mountain safely. The car cannot reach the destination with the way you have been driving it till now.

You do know what to do. You know that you need to conserve the gas. The only purpose of the gas is to move the car along with all the essentials needed to be carried with it. Currently the car is dragging all the excess weight of the food, drinks, clothes, and the camping gear. The things which were making your journey very enjoyable so far suddenly seem to be a liability. All it matters now is that you reach the destination safely and in time. You decide to remove everything non-essential from the car. You throw away the baggage, picnic chair and everything that is adding to the weight. You also throw all excess food and drinks because you know you will get more of it once you reach to the top. Every extra weight costs you more gas and you do not want to waste it at all. As you lighten the car, the chances of you reaching to the top improve.

You know that you are still quite far from reaching to the top. You have thrown all the non-essentials and made the car as light as it could be. Yet, you are riding comfortably and enjoying your ride. You realize that the environment control and the music system load the car's engine too. Therefore, you shut off the air-conditioner and switch the radio off. You open the windows to make you comfortable with the natural air outside. You let go your comforts to allow every bit of the gas towards making the car move forward. When you come across a junction on the road, you know that you do not want the scenic route which takes a little longer path. You do not have the luxury of comfortable ride. You want to reach the destination taking the shortest path even though it might be a jerky ride along the dirt road.

Those who wish to seek the goal of total perception must know that their goal too is at the top of a very high mountain of life, and they are currently travelling heavily loaded while enjoying the comfort of their ride and the beauty of the surroundings. The fuel of life is limited, and the time and energy are not going to be enough to be wasted on all non-essentials. One can either reach the destination by travelling light, conserving all energy into one direction and taking a direct route or can continue enjoying the beauty and comforts of the world and wasting the fuel and making sure that the destination will never be reached.

Everything drains the energy, whether it is our habit of reading the newspaper, watching television, reading fictional stories, collecting information, gaining (worldly) knowledge, partying and networking, chatting and gossiping, or working hard in workplaces to earn money and gather comforts of life. It does not matter whether one watches television for entertainment or for education, sports, or politics; it requires one's attention and therefore drains energy. The fact is that any new input to the mind starts a chain reaction of thousands of new thoughts which continue to trap and engage the mind for many days, weeks or months or sometimes, even the whole lifetime. Ignorant of the ways of the mind, we do not just feed one or two inputs, but thousands of new inputs in form of information every day for long hours. The amount of energy being wasted by our minds every day is unimaginable. Can one even imagine how much energy is made available to us when all this wasted energy is saved by throwing the extra luggage and switching off the non-essential luxury habits? What would you think this abundant energy do when it is saved from being wasted? The difference in this collected energy and an ordinary energy is the same as that of a torch light and a laser gun. The difference between the two is the same as the fire from a blow torch and the fire from a rocket's exhaust. While the ordinary energy allows one to live a life, the other one helps one to transcend into the higher dimension. The best part is that one need not do anything special to figure out how to achieve this. The energy is knowledge itself; it knows its way!

The main reason for waste of useful energy is multiplicity. A laser is a coherent beam; all its energy is directed in a single direction. It is our tendency to get involved with multiple things at a time that makes our efforts insincere. Our minds are involved in multiple issues all the time. Yet, no single tendency of mind is bad as long as it is the only thing one is concerned about. If you are busy cutting wood, then this sole task itself can make someone achieve total perception. Those who teach spirituality tell you that desires and attachments are barriers to your progress. It is not entirely true! It is the multiple desires and multiple attachments that drain your energy. If you had only one desire, whatever it might be, it will work miracles for you. Those who wish to make a lot of money and are driven by only this single desire, end up being rich. The important thing to note here is that the desire should be pure, single, and not corrupted by additional sub-desires. Likewise, if one needs to drop all the desires (as learned from reading scriptures and listening to people of knowledge), one still needs one single desire; the desire to get rid of all desires. One cannot achieve anything unless there was one sincere desire. It is not the absence of desires, attachments, or removal of all your vices, but the coherence of one single action that works for you. A single concentrated effort can achieve any seemingly impossible target because it collects all your available energies in a single direction.

Those who wish to make significant progress in any field, not just spirituality, must learn to become single-pointed. At any time, one must be busy with only one thing. If one is taking bath, then the only thing one must be doing is to bathe. There is an immense joy in bathing. If you did not think about anything at the time of taking bath, you would be mesmerized by the wonderful experiences of water, soap, bubbles and the feeling of relaxation that would usually be missing from the rest of the day in action. When you are driving your car to the work, you need to only drive the car and be aware of everything that goes on around you. It is difficult for most of us because once the mind learns something, it takes over the action and lets you enjoy other activities. Therefore, we tend to get ourselves busy with thoughts of past or future while driving with the sound or music from the radio running in the background. Can you see the immense drainage of our energies? We are never aware of our journey on the routes that we are habitual of taking every day. It is only when we reach the destination, we realize that we had driven the way without registering that we actually drove through that path! (Mind Trick: Next time when you start driving off to or from work or on a route that you always take, take a random turn without planning. Notice the change to your awareness!)

The problem is not that we do not try to do only one thing at any time. The problem is that we think doing multiple tasks at the same time is a desirable skill. People are proud of doing many things at a time. They feel they are utilizing their time in an efficient way. That is understandable in the worldly state of things. The reality is that by indulging in multiple activities, we are not doing any single task in a complete manner. The way in which total perception is a possibility. It is not just about the tasks; we do not even know how to entertain ourselves with full attention. People have a habit of watching movies or eating their favorite food while browsing through their phones or computers. Our approach of getting any job done with an average attention leads us to live a mediocre life. This is good enough for a torch light but not anywhere close to a laser beam.

A Total Perception only is possible when
1. *We are not doing multiple tasks.*
2. *We are not thinking or past or planning for future.*
3. *We are not unduly busy with useless activities.*

Dependence on Knowledge

Our knowledge is the biggest barrier towards Total Perception.

In his book, "The Psychology of Science", Maslow wrote, "I suppose it is tempting, if the only tool you have is a hammer, to treat everything as if it were a nail." We all have a tool; it is called the Mind. Therefore, the most we must be capable of, is what the Mind has capability of doing. Mind has an ability to observe, look for patterns, remember them, assign a symbolic name or idea to the pattern, and recall the existing information in terms of story and experience whenever needed. Mind can imagine or act only based on memory of the past. It cannot come up with anything new and fresh. Something new and fresh has no pattern that the Mind knows of.

Imagine the world of ants. Let's think about an ant who is very intelligent and wants to transcend beyond the present bounds and limitations of its physical manifestation in this world. In a hot desert, it lives under the scorching earth in the cool place with the large population of other ants. It comes out of its cool place in search of food and must return back either with or without food within a time interval of ten minutes. If it fails to return to its house, it would be dehydrated and choked to death in the extreme heat. If an ant were to contemplate and figure out how to transcend and go beyond its physical or mental capabilities, what might it come up with? Would it not wonder if it could somehow be able to spend more than an hour in the heat? It could possibly try to look for or invent some protective sheet that it could cover its body while it hunted for food. It could somehow look for a special kind of food that could hydrate it much better to allow it to sustain longer hours outside its home. Whatever it might try, its attempts will always remain in the realm of an ant-world. It is an ant, and every attempt will have a limitation that an ant must have. Will it ever try to imagine or solve the problems that other cockroaches, snakes, flies or even humans have?

We too suffer from the same limitation, the limitation of our knowledge. This knowledge is the collection of information that we have stored in our minds since we were born. This knowledge is the knowledge of the whole mankind. Though we may feel proud to have the highest intelligence in this universe on account of this knowledge, we must know that the same knowledge also presents a hindrance to knowing anything new and fresh. Our minds cannot cope with new things, new ideas or new information. Unless the new information can be perceived in relation to some (previously) known pattern or a symbol, it is meaningless to the mind. In the same way, in absence of any (previously collected) information related to the new observation, mind finds itself helpless to deal with it. It must deal the new in terms of the old. It is same as trying to hit everything with it meets with a hard blow because it knows nothing beyond a hammer.

Our brain stores all our learning and experiences, good as well as bad. It uses this memory of past snapshots in all its future dealings. It is a good way to exist in this world because it helps one to safeguard from what was perceived as a danger in the past. It also helps sustain, grow, and enjoy life because one tries to repeatedly do what yielded itself a great satisfaction in the past. The mechanical way of existing in this way has become a habit for all of us. Our dependence on knowledge is a great way for our physical survival but a very dumb way for our inherent intelligent quality. The cosmos is presenting millions of new experiences every day, yet we are living a monotonous life repeating same actions each day of our life. We get up, take a shower, eat breakfast, go to office, come back home, eat dinner, watch television, read newspaper, spend some time with our children and go to sleep. This is the most common way most of middle-class population lives their lives. In the process of evaluating every new experience in terms of our past knowledge, we miss the chance of living a fresh joy, excitement, mystery or wonder from our lives.

Once my neighbor Madhavan shared this with me. He said, "It has been almost twenty years living in America. When we came, our kids were very young. By now, they have already finished their college education. One afternoon I and my wife decided to clean their room where countless toys, dolls and games were still stuffed in the shelves since the last twenty years. As we continued to pick one piece after another, we were surprised to find many of games which we had completely forgotten. We remembered a few of those games which were very exciting, and we all had a great fun playing together. There were many interesting things that were gifted to our kids on their birthdays by their friends but were never yet opened. While we were planning to drop all the stuff at a donation center, we thought we could keep the best ones for our next-door neighbor's child. I dropped a quick message to my neighbor asking if she would like to have some of the games to see if their kid found them interesting. I was visualizing how excited the kid would be to find an unexpected delivery of some exciting play stuff. Within five minutes, I got a response from my neighbor saying that they had a few board games already and their kids were not much into playing them."

Madhavan was shocked to see why someone would not want to at least have a look into what new opportunity was being presented! Especially when there was no risk, nothing to lose! Was it anything but a stupid convenience on his neighbor's part assuming that we might dump a few boring board games in their house? It was clear that the mind had depended on its existing knowledge that all board games are boring, and he might bring the same boring games which their kids never had interest in. The mind had opted for a security, imagined a known scenario, and quickly made a decision. We all play this trick hundreds of times every day. Every moment we avoid uncertainty and rely on our memories and experiences to decide our future actions. We do not experience reality at all. Instead, we live a completely imagined and fabricated version of reality. We remain untouched of reality because we are too afraid of uncertainty and reality is nothing but that. Our knowledge is a great tool for our survival but is also a huge barrier to all the excitement and mysteries of the unknown universe.

Spirituality is about going beyond our current limitations and transcending into the realm of unknown. But when it comes to unknown, our minds have no use. With no mind to our rescue, we must deal with the unknown with something we have no experience from our past memory. This is our limitation, as to how do we do anything about something where we do not know what to do about it and how to do anything. We find this dependence on knowledge blocking our efforts when we are asked to practice meditation. The simplest instruction that a teacher gives to the students is about sitting quietly without trying to think or do anything. This very simple instruction is the most difficult task for the mind because the mind knows only one thing - to think! There is no way the mind can keep itself from not thinking, because it is something it does not know. Moreover, it also knows only one thing, that is to do something. It does not know what it means not to do something. Any effort not to do becomes paradoxical because an effort means doing something. With its current toolbox called the mind, and its tools of thoughts, actions, memories and expectations, humans find it hard to transcend the mind and to know something which is beyond the grasps of their minds.

> *A ticket-checker working in a movie theater was having tooth pain. He went to a dentist. The Dentist made him sit in the chair and asked him if he could identify which tooth hurt. The ticket-checker said, "Upper Balcony, first row, third from left."*

A person's dependence on (existing) knowledge also affects his or her ability to observe anything with a fresh 'look.' If one wishes to know completely about one's own nature and the nature of universe around it, one needs to have an acute sense of perception. One cannot know about something if one cannot see it completely, or touch it completely or smell, taste or hear it completely. Even though, having a complete and thorough perception through our five senses would not be sufficient to understand the world totally, but it would at least, be a good start. Yet, our current limitation is that we depend on our previous experiences to observe new encounters with the universe. If we are asked simply to look at a tree without naming, analyzing, describing, or expecting, we find it extremely difficult as well as a completely useless activity. It is our big weakness that we cannot perceive anything unless it is also accompanied by a thought process. The thoughts are nothing but using memory to bring names and forms into our awareness and associate the current perception with our past. It may seem a bit harsh, but unless someone has 'trained' oneself to discard the mind and get to know how to observe without bringing in any previous knowledge, one is very far from (realizing) the true knowledge of one's own self and the nature of reality around oneself.

If you have read some scriptures, heard some wise ones or attended some sermons, you would have come across this strange idea that the best approach to solving the most complex situations is by knowing that you do not know anything. This comes as a surprisingly strange and counter-intuitive approach! How could you solve a problem by not knowing anything about it? We have been trained with the idea that the more a person studies, the smarter he or she becomes. You would read or hear it countless times everywhere about the good habit or reading books. We all love to talk about the CEOs and Presidents on how many books they read. To us, the knowledge is the way to wisdom, not otherwise. This is the trap of the Mind. This is the ultimate barrier to Total Perception. It is because between you and the perceived sensation, there comes the knowledge, the knowledge of names, symbols, identities and memory.

> *A Total Perception only is possible when*
> 1. *We stop behaving based on our preconceived notions.*
> 2. *We are able to look anything new without a prior knowledge.*
> 3. *We embrace uncertainty wholeheartedly.*
> 4. *We embrace, "I do not know" approach*

Stuck with the Past

Unable to forget, forgive and let go.

We thrive on our memory. It is a great way to survive and grow on this planet among many dangers and threats such as predators, natural calamities, and hunger. The memory allows the creatures to continue those activities which yielded rewards in the past as well as avoid those which caused pain or threat to their lives. Among all other creatures, we humans have relied greatest on memory and have used it as the most important tool given to us by the nature. We depend on our memory so much that we cannot imagine our lives without it. We fear losing our memory and along with it everything that we built in this world of ours including our name, identity, relations, views, and beliefs.

It is not short of some tragedy that the greatest tool which ensures our survival and continued growth in this world also makes us conditioned, mechanical, and reactive in our behavior towards other human beings. We have used our power to remember so much that we do not and cannot drop this habit even when we have no threat to our survival. The fact is that we have made our lives so much safer and comfortable that we do not need to depend on our memories as much as humans might have needed a few thousand years ago. We do not live in jungles where we have to struggle for food, shelter and protection every minute of our lives. Yet, we spend most of our time in this world utilizing every possible moment of our lives occupied with memories, knowledge, and accumulated experiences of the past.

It is true that we cannot possibly survive in this world without memory. We need to do our jobs, go to market or other places, interact with different people and do hundreds of chores which require using our memories. If we were completely aware and using our memory only to the extent that allows us to conduct our livelihood smoothly in this world, there is absolutely no problem. But we have taken this valuable tool too far and shut our doors of perception through excessive attachment to our memory.

Our special abilities to remember people and their (past) behavior allows us to plan our strategies with them in future. We burden ourselves with our relations and interaction so much that we strongly need to remember every single event with every single person we give importance. Our need to remember people and their behavior towards us or others does not let us forget. When we do not forget, we take a finite amount of space in our brains towards remembering such things. The more data we keep in our brains to remember, the more burden we put on our brain to maintain such memory and retrieve it to use it in our daily behavior. If we were to design a machine to do something like this, we know what it would mean in terms of the machine's performance. The increasing amount of data in storages will continue to slow down the machine's ability to process current data. This is what happens when we do not forget, do not forgive and let go, so as to release the data from memory and lighten it. The more we free the memory from remembering useless information, the more receptive our mind would become to perceive new information available to it every moment.

Let us see how the world becomes if we do not let memory of our past experiences come in way of fresh perceptions. When we meet a person, if we do not carry any other memory than the subtle fact that the person has a certain identity and a certain relationship with us, we become open to noticing something that we would never have noticed.

You are taking a walk in the garden when a person seems to approach from far. Immediately you recognize him as Bob, who is your son's class teacher. You have two options. As the first option, you could immediately remember how he had not been very friendly whenever you had a parent-teacher meeting with him. Even though your kid has left the school long time ago, you carry the bitter memories about his behavior and your emotions about how he should have treated your son. With those memories in background, you look at that person and therefore let the rest of the universe get disappeared from your perception for a few minutes. Alternatively, you could let your memory and past experience take a back seat and simply notice the physical appearance in front of you with the backdrop of your memories about him as well as everything else such as the people, birds, trees, animals, sounds and the smell in the air. If you observe, you will notice that you have not dropped your memories completely but have only allowed them to take a back seat. In the second alternative, the memories do not let your emotions drive your behavior. Instead, the awareness of your emotions on watching the teacher makes you forget, forgive, and move on in a short period of time. In future encounters, you would observe that you do not have any emotions left in you about this person even though the memories still remain. Being aware of our memories and the emotions they bring, we not only forget and release those memories from the brain's burden, but also allow the brain to start perceiving the surroundings and remain seated in the present moment.

You might say what is such a big deal about not being aware in once-in-a-while event as just described here. The problem is that unawareness such as this does not just happen occasionally. Instead, we continue to remain unaware and therefore, miss the present moment in almost every moment. This is because, the moment we get away from this one incident, our next encounter with something or someone is also going to be the same. We will meet or notice another person or people and immediately our memory, experiences and past emotions will drive our next course of action. Continuing this way, our inability to drop our past experiences and our never-ending dependence on those experiences to guide our (future) behavior ensures that we never perceive the world ever in its real form. Almost all the times, we will continue to miss the world out there!

When it comes to forgetting, we think that we need to only forget (and therefore forgive) our bad experiences with people. This is not true. We need to be forgetting all good as well as bad experiences if we want to explore the world with fresh eyes every moment. Like the bad experiences where we try to ignore, avoid, or contradict those people who had not been in good terms with us in the past, the good experiences also put a veil in front of our eyes. Just because we liked someone's behavior in the past, we tend to put our confidence in all their future dealings with us. This means that with such tendency of ours we stop perceiving our new experiences with a complete awareness and we let our past knowledge create a pre-built picture about future encounters. Each one of us has many such experiences where we find we were cheated or deceived by someone. People or entities can only cheat or deceive us when we had believed them some time in the past. We only believe someone when we have had some good or favorable experience with them in the past. It all comes to a single fact; our dependence on good or bad experiences of the past blind us to all our future endeavors with the universe due to our secession of perceptions.

A Total Perception only is possible when
　　1. We do not remain stuck to bad or good experiences.

Questions & Challenges

We are afraid of questions, whether asking or responding.

Our universe is full of mystery and suspense. Every moment we are faced with countless uncertainties which would normally make us act either with fear or with caution. It is a different thing that we do not acknowledge this fact and continue to live our lives with a blind conviction that everything is under our control. We also believe that anything that is not yet in our control will sooner or later be in our control due to the continuous efforts of our civilization. As a result, we continue to live our lives being much careless and ignorant of our intuitions and perceptions. This behavior of ours is evident in the way we react to problems, challenges, and questions in our lives.

There are two fundamental reasons why someone might ask questions. A question can mean that the questioner is interested in exploring more on the subject by trying to collect additional information. At the same time, a question can also be a means of denying and resisting the current situation. When I ask why I must close the door always, I might either be interested in knowing the reason for always having to close the door, or I might be trying to resist my having to close the door. It is quite probable that a question is of the second type that forces most people to create a wall of defense around themselves. When we think that someone is denying or resisting something (because they have questioned us), we may either get offended or may see that our efforts of explaining the situation might not be easily acceptable to the other party. When there is a high possibility of the question to be a complaint or a resistance, we may as well avoid the situations when people ask us questions. It is also possible that when someone does ask us a question genuinely, we might respond in an offensive tone or rudely because we have already assumed a denial or a resistance in the asking of such a question.

We are so deeply obsessed with our own image in the eyes of others that we do not want to leave any ground uncovered which might expose our weaknesses or limitations. We are defensive about our shortcomings not only because it shows us in a bad light, but also that once they get exposed, we might have to work and fix them. This means that most of the times we ourselves are not aware of our problems and yet, we do not want to know (about) them. We fear the discomfort of possibly destroying the feeling of being safe and comfortable in our own little cocoon of (false) security. Questions open the scope of the unknown. Mind is fearful of the unknown and would do anything to avoid having to deal with the fear and uncertainties. This leads us to behave in all possible strange ways and makes it hard for us to perceive completely all that we come to face.

> *Once an inspector visited a school and went to a class to find what the students knew about Ramayana. He asked a kid who broke Shiva's bow. The kid had no idea. He got scared and said, "Please believe me. I didn't do it!"*

We ask questions for various reasons. Questions are the way to explore and get to know our universe and its intriguing mysteries. It is through asking and investigating deep enough only that we can gain knowledge. Understanding ourselves and the world this way can help us become wiser. Yet, settled deep into our own insecurities, we have changed the interpretations of questions completely. Our minds have a very special relation with challenges and problems. There is no way we can face a problem and remain with it without either avoiding it, denying it, or trying to solve it. We have habituated ourselves such that when we face someone's questions, we become cautious of their motives. We take questions as a problem, and therefore react the same way as we would to a problem or a challenge. It is not easy to ask someone a question and simply get a response. There is always a possibility for you being misjudged, misinterpreted, or seen with a suspicion for asking a question.

Once Martha shared her experience with me. She told me that in the organization where she worked, the CEO used to deliver a speech to company employees at the end of every quarter presenting the company's results and communicating the goals and expectations for the coming quarters. At the end of the meeting, he used to invite employees to ask questions. Unless the questioner simply praised the company's results or made some general remarks, the CEO always seemed to respond as if the purpose of the question was a way of passing an opinion or judgement. For example, when someone asked why our company purchased a new company, the CEO seemed to interpret it as if according to the questioner our company should not have made the purchase. He used to justify the company's acts rather than explaining the rationales used in coming up with the decisions to purchase the new company.

Srinivasan's one of close friends was very obsessed with Karnatic music. He once asked his friend what exactly he liked in Karnatic music. Quite unexpectedly, his friend took this question as a passing judgment that there could be nothing likeable in the Karnatic music.

We not only respond strangely to the questions asked to us but also hesitate in asking questions. The universe is a great mystery, and it cannot be understood unless we question everything around us. There are countless things and phenomena that we do not know about. We not only not ask questions or try to understand the things that do not make sense, but we also continue to get going as if it does not matter. We do not ask questions to others if they are elders or superior to us fearing that they might get offended. We do not ask questions to those who are younger to us fearing that our ignorance might be exposed. We do not ask questions to our colleagues, friends, and relative fearing that that they might get offended and it might hurt our future relations with us. We do not ask questions to those who are running government, those who are managing our organizations and various others who are in charge of making laws and regulations. We continue to live a second-hand life not trying to offend anyone by shutting all our curiosities and living with the existing inconveniences in this world.

A Total Perception only is possible when
1. *We are not resisting questions and problems.*
2. *We are comfortable with questions and not necessarily trying to find answers for every question.*
3. *When we start questioning everyone and everything.*

10

Need of Safety

Our Fears hinder our Perception

Our minds register our everyday experiences in memory. It is important for our safe existence because our memories make us to avoid all those situations which we remember as painful and dangerous from our past experiences. On the other hand, our memories of good times help us repeat our past actions repeatedly in future to gain the same advantages again and again. As we grow older, our habitual dependence on our memories makes us rely less and less on our sense organs. With reduced use of our senses, we find ourselves unable to register the changes happening in our surroundings the way we should. Instead, we make excessive use of our memories and past experiences because it provides us with simpler, faster, and safer decision making for most of our life events.

Our undue dependence on memory might make our lives very efficient, but it also deprives us of our ability to sense and know our universe as it happens in the present moment. With such approach (of using our memories), our ability to know the present moment is not straightforward. Instead, it is wrapped with many kinds of fears and uncertainties. When we approach a rose plant, we are cautious of the possible thorns on its branch. When we approach a wet surface, we are careful not to slip and fall. We ride our bikes with helmets, go out in the sun with sunglasses and sunscreens and walk on earth wearing comfortable shoes.

Our fears do not let us experience the universe as direct or truthfully as it could be. We do not drink water from any random place or eat some fruit directly by pulling it off from a tree. We cover our nose when walking past a heap of garbage. We cannot stand someone's anger or disgust or abuse. We either avoid or run away from there or fight back with counter abuse to feel better. Our all encounters with the real world have a strong influence of our insecurities and fears. We do not want to face anything that might make us feel bad, inconvenient, or insecure. If we come across such situations, we try to flee or avoid it immediately. It is not a total or complete perception that we are interested at any time. It is only the pleasant perceptions that we care about.

Fear is what we are! We are not just our bodies. We are a whole complex set of our thinking, ideologies, expectations, sufferings, desires, experiences, and memories. We not only remain burdened with the weight of our such heavy existence, but also remain fearful of losing any of this payload from our heads. This constant fear of losing what we are makes us observe this universe under constant pressure. This pressure is very similar to the constant force of gravity that our bodies experience at all the times. We become so habituated of this (gravitational) force that we never feel that in any position, the part in contact with the earth is compressed and pushed down by the weight of the body. Just like we are completely unaware of such a pressure and are completely comfortable sitting or lying down, we have become oblivious of our fears and insecurities which affect our ability to know and observe our surroundings.

We are afraid of not letting go all that we have accumulated. We love to be a part of our social relations and feel secure in the company of our relatives, friends, colleagues, and neighbors. With the desire to continue enjoying the closeness of our acquaintance comes the insecurities and fears of losing such benefits. Such insecurity makes us behave in constrained ways. When we speak, we try to use words very carefully so as not to hurt the other. When we listen, we try to ignore harsh and angered words from those whom we love dearly, so as not to damage our relationships. When we touch someone, we are cautious not to exhibit certain unintended motives or improper behavior. Our every act of perceiving the world of relations around ourselves is seriously affected by the fears of losing what we have accumulated over a long time. Being fearful and approaching everything and everybody carefully, we lose the chance of perceiving the universe in a total and complete manner.

Amanda was rock-climbing alone. It had become dark by the time she had almost made to the top. Suddenly her grip loosened, and she slipped a long distance toward the valley to finally get engaged with the safety clip. She kept hanging in the dark with no idea how far she might be from the ground below. She spent the whole night hanging on to the rope to finally figure out in the morning that she was only five feet from the ground.

We are afraid of the unknown. We cannot move until we know where we are going. We need to know the direction, the purpose, and the goal. This very need to know is the enemy of perception. When you want to know, then you stop perceiving and start interpreting all that your senses register. If you hear a sound, you are not hearing but trying to understand what it means. If what you hear does not make sense, you ignore it for as long as it continues. This sound then becomes a background noise that you do not seem to hear even though it always reaches your ears. If you stop right now and start listening to the sounds around you, you will notice that there are at least fifty different sounds that are reaching your ears, but your mind does not care to listen. Our habitual ignoring of all the sounds that do not seem to have any purpose for us makes them go away from our perceptions. Ignoring everything that does not make sense gives a sense of security to the mind. It goes restless if it encounters something that it cannot understand.

We are afraid of letting go all that we have accumulated. We have accumulated our own personality, our identity over our complete lifetime. Our identity is made of all our achievements, our belongings, our fames, our fears, sorrows and insecurities and our opinions and beliefs. It is the biggest investment of our lives and with all this payload we continue to enjoy (or suffer) the benefits of our existence in the world as who we are. While we have amassed such a huge load of our personalities or identity, we do not feel bothered by the hardship of having to carry around us all the time. On the contrary, we remain fearful of losing any of our accumulations. Surprisingly, it is not just our pleasures, blessings, or precious belongings that we are afraid of losing, but even our pains, sufferings, and hardships that we do not want to lose. Having invested so heavily in our own personality and identity, we continue to perceive the universe with great caution and fear. When trying to attempt doing anything, we are fearful of doing any mistake in front of others. Despite our cautious approach, when someone points our mistakes, we completely miss the opportunity to observe and watch. In the fear of losing our reputation, we defend, react, and counter with an argument every time something wrong happens, and someone talks about it. Our fears never let us see the things as they are. We remain fearful of ugliness and pain in this world and continue to struggle trying to avoid such experiences.

> *A Total Perception only is possible when*
> 1. *We become aware of who we are.*
> 2. *We are comfortable with the unknown and uncertain.*
> 3. *We are comfortable with letting go.*
> 4. *We understand that there is no real security in life Ever.*

Unaware of Change

Ignoring Warning Signs

The universe is brilliant. The existence is mysterious. There is no end to moments new wonders cannot be uncovered. We as humans have the most advantage of discovering the hidden secrets and enjoying the breathtaking beauty of the nature. We have an advantage compared to any other of species not because of having superior sense organs, but because of our developed brains and its ability to use intellect. The brain allows interpretation of perceived information in much detail which allows us safer and more comfortable life on this planet.

It is a kind of universal rule that nobody is ever best in all areas. While our abilities of our brains allow us to visualize our future growth, security, and comfort, it also makes us lose sight of the present. At every moment we sense our surroundings through the different sense organs. Yet, we fail to pay attention to any of our perceptions because we are preoccupied with unlimited mental activities. Asking someone to simply have a cup of tea and not to do anything else is a huge problem. People cannot just let one or more of their senses take over and keep their minds relaxed for few moments. Just having a tea or coffee without talking to someone or reading a book or watching a television program seems like an utter waste of time!

Our minds which are always avoiding the present moment lose the opportunity to notice subtle changes going around them. These changes are so insignificant that the mind does not bother to register them. Our minds are always focused on the bigger, bolder, faster, louder movements around them because they are important for the survival. With such tendencies to ignore slower, milder, and smaller changes around us, we lose the opportunity to perceive the universe in its completeness.

It is not that we are helpless, and we simply lose the opportunity to perceive the grand universe without any outside help available to us. On the contrary, the universe gives us great many warning signals to remind us, but we fail to pay attention. If we were attentive, we would know of the missed opportunities of being perceptive to our surroundings. We all know how soon we become accustomed of driving our cars on familiar routes without needing to pay attention to our actual act of driving. It is only after we have completely driven and reached a certain place that we realize that we have no memory of our driving on the road or having passed from the places without remembering about them. It seems no less than a miracle to see how our mind and body continues to take control of the complex mechanisms of steering, braking, or speeding the vehicle along with other important tasks of taking care of the road signs, traffic lights, pedestrians, and other cars.

We have known about this helplessness of ours about not being aware when driving on the familiar routes. This is one of those subtle warning signals that we have noticed so many times that we have accepted it as normal. We do not get surprised or worried about our driving the cars or bikes completely unconscious. We go even a step further and make our mind even more negligent by listening to audio books, music or news, or by enjoying a drink or talking to the fellow passengers or talking over the phone to some friend during driving. We do anything and everything possible to do anything but to pay attention to things worth noticing. If we did not engage in any activity other than the actual driving, we might actually be looking at the road, feeling the shaking, vibrating and bumping of our seats, feeling the touch and the smell of the leather seats, noticing the boredom or tiredness of our bodies and hundreds of other things that our senses might find worth noticing during the drive. It is not that we are unable to perceive the universe totally, it is that we consciously choose to ignore the magical universe for the satisfaction and pleasure of our lazy, restless, and mischievous minds.

One of the other warning signals we have become habitual of is pain. We all have hurt ourselves and experienced pain in our bodies many times. When there is no pain in our body, we do not feel its presence. We never feel our fingers, toes, tongue, skin, or eyes in our everyday life. Yet, a small thorn on the tip of our thumb or a speck of dust in our eyes can make it difficult to take our attention away from it. As long as our thumbs can feel the pain, we experience the inconvenience and pain during anything else we do such as reading, eating or relaxing. Yet, when the pain goes away, we go back to our usual life completely ignorant of our bodies and their perfectly healthy state. The occasional pains in our bodies are the warning signs that can make us aware of all the kinds of perceptions that we are unaware of in our life. We are hardly aware of our breathing, our heartbeat, vibrations in our bodies and many more sensations that could be noticed if we paid attention. It is only when we are breathless or are given big shocks that the discomfort makes us aware of their presence.

We do not know what we have never seen, heard, or known about. We can know about the universe and its feel either through a direct perception or through using our minds to know from the experience of others. It is true that we can feel pain ourselves but cannot feel the pain that others experience. Yet, having known how our bodies react in pain, our minds can somehow figure out the presence of pain in others too. The way we pull our hands away from fire, and then start rubbing the part which gets exposed to heat we come to know of pain in others if they seem to be exhibiting similar bodily reactions. If we see someone lying on the road and shaking vigorously in a pool of blood, we can understand the pain the other body must be going through even though none of our senses record any pain. Despite such intelligence of our minds in recognizing pain in others through our own experiences, we are unable to realize the truth of death by noticing the same in others. We see people dying around us but live a life as if we will never die. Our all actions, reactions and emotions are based on our permanent presence in this universe. Living in a dynamically changing world, with many new bodies being born every moment and many dying every moment, we continue to miss the beauty of the life as well as death.

> *A Total Perception only is possible when*
> 1. *We are able to notice warning signs.*
> 2. *We can notice the weaknesses of the Mind to fall for bold and beautiful and go beyond it.*

12

Dropping Out Early

Most people do not go all the way because they are satisfied with the limited results already achieved.

We have existed on this planet for hundreds of thousands of years and have come a long way since our initial times of struggle for existence among other wild creatures and cruel natural calamities. We have been able to make use of the highly developed human brain to achieve all that we imagined for ourselves, the security, the comfort, and countless ways of entertaining ourselves. We are programmed to go after that which gives us more pleasure and lesser pain just like any other living creature. Despite all our abilities which makes us superior compared to any other living life on this planet, we are far from experiencing true wisdom. A true wisdom can only exist in form of absolute knowledge, and an absolute knowledge cannot exist without a total perception. All that matters is a state of total perception; Any state close to that is still incomplete.

> *Reema looked very excited! Someone asked her why. She said she was 'this' close to becoming millionaire. All the numbers in her lottery ticket were just one number less than the winning numbers!*

It is not our special abilities that are to be blamed for our inability to perceive our universe completely, but our weaknesses that we fail to notice in our daily activities. We fail to observe many of our habits as weaknesses because we do achieve most of everything we desire and therefore get satisfied with the results we achieve in our attempts. Our biggest mistake is that we never go all the way in our quest to achieve anything. We get satisfied at a certain stage and then quit our journey so that we can reap the benefits of our efforts. In almost all the cases in our present human lives, we stop our journey of learning and developing the moment we start getting financial returns greater than our imagination. It is the fundamental nature of the mind to run around in search for happiness, and to come to a halt when the sensation of happiness is perceived.

It is true that we do not go all the way. It is also true that it is not practical to go all the way. Going all the way is another way of saying that someone wants to achieve perfection. A perfect state is an illusion. There is nothing perfect in universe. We all can strive for perfection, but we do not ever achieve it. What we achieve is the best possible and practical level of being as close to the perfect state as possible. A perfect state is unachievable and to achieve it means that one continues to pursue this goal for ever. A total perception is one such perfect state. One cannot hope to reach a state of total perception if one is overly satisfied with the fruits achieved halfway through the journey. The reason most people cannot meet the God is that when after a long and tiring journey they are presented with the pleasures of the heaven, they are overjoyed with satisfaction of rewards and do not see any reason to pursue their journey. They are afraid that they might forfeit the rewards they were presented, had they continued to go towards their ultimate goal without getting interested in those rewards.

The readers might not agree with me. It is such an absurd thing, they would think! Why would I say that most people are happy to leave the things halfway and do not pursue anything till the end? One would need to give some serious thought to our lives and see if it is not the case. Do we continue to educate ourselves for ever or do we stop at certain time when we think we have collected enough credentials to stop learning and start earning money? Do we continue to train ourselves in playing tennis, swimming, running on the tracks or do we get out of the training mode and enter playing for championships and competitions? We would never continue doing anything till the very end. An end is an illusion! It is never achieved. It is a state of perfection. One would never continue to play tennis or drive car for ever. At certain time, it would be worth losing the huge rewards of dropping away from the practice and start earning money from the skills achieved so far.

A total perception is the state of perfection. The journey towards achieving a state of total perception is an endless one. The human mind cannot foresee the true rewards of the final stage just as one cannot imagine what it must be like meeting the God itself when presented with an opportunity to enjoy the pleasures of heaven halfway on the route. In almost all the cases, whoever starts the journey to achieve total perception, cannot continue all the way because the rewards already achieved in the journey are enough to provide all the comforts and pleasures one could ever imagine. The moment one stops the journey and starts reaping the benefits of the journey so far, any hope of getting to know the total perception is lost.

Spirituality is very different from anything the Mind can know. There is no end (to achieve). There are no results. However, a mind cannot be interested in anything that has no purpose or no goal in sight. This is why when a pursuer starts getting unexpected results far before he or she is able to get a grasp of the (ultimate) knowledge, there is no reason to continue towards boring and senseless activities for uncertain periods. It appears as if all the hard work towards spiritual growth finally paid of in terms of a better (worldly) life. We have hundreds of examples around us. They all had started seriously towards pursuing their inner growth. But at some point of time, their popularity made them drift away from their path and change their profession into delivering motivational speeches and writing books to earn money.

A Total Perception only is possible when
1. *You are aware that there are no material rewards in the end.*
2. *You are left with absolutely no expectations or hope.*

13

Poor Judgment

When forced to make a correction, we end up picking even worse alternative.

We are living in a state of flux, where situations change dynamically, and we have multiple options to choose at every moment. However, most of our adult life goes on smoothly because we have learnt to continue with the choices which have worked fairly well in the past. Even though the life continues to change at a fast pace, we tend to live a fairly stable life because of our habit to stick to our way of making decisions. Having lost the ability to choose proper alternatives due to our lazy approach of living our life, when the time does come where we are forced to make a decision, we tend to pick an alternative which is worse than the original situation.

Mr Gupta went for a trip to hills with his family. He booked a room with two double beds. He was accompanied with his wife and two teenage kids, a son and a daughter. Since it would be improper allowing the teenage son and the daughter to share the same bed, he came up with a better option. He slept with his daughter while his wife slept with the boy!

This is what we do everyday in our life. When we hear about one presidential candidate's affairs or lies, we immediately choose the other candidate. This looks completely reasonable to us. All we want is to avoid the present choice because we are uncomfortable with one particular defect. We do not care what we are choosing as an alternative and that there might be five other defects far more serious than the present one. That question does not even arise. When we find our current boyfriend cheating, we immediately switch to the next person. We do not wait to see if the other choice is worthy of our selection. That question does not arise. All we want is to avoid the present disaster. When we do not like our current Supervisor, we immediately switch our department, or our company. We do not wait to see if the other choice is a better one. We do not find it important at the moment of running away from the current crises where we are going. All we care is that we go to any other place than the current one. And in all this heat of avoiding crisis, we jump into a bigger trouble, a worse choice.

This happens every time we have to avoid an undesired alternative. We unknowingly pick up even worse option because our attention is completely on avoiding the current disaster. We fail to notice the quality of alternative that we pick up unknowingly. When some of us get attracted towards the goodness of spirituality and start listening to knowledgeable teachers, influencers, or saints, we fall in the same trap. It is no doubt a wonderful change in our lives that we start paying attention to our ignorance, weaknesses, and unawareness and therefore, seek a path toward (achieving) intelligence and self-awareness. Yet, our tragedy is that in our attempt for avoiding the trap of ignorance, we fall for even bigger trap. That trap is of getting stuck to the first alternative we encounter when looking around for help and guidance. Most of such inquisitive minds get hold of their favorite teacher and end their journey right there. They start attending their preaching sessions either online or in person. A few others get into a habit of strict schedule of yoga and breathing exercises. It is interesting to note that there is not much difference in the level of ignorance between their previous habit of living ignorantly and the newly acquired habit of pursuing imagined spiritual intelligence. As suggested in the example in the beginning, the new habit formed by such spiritual seekers is far more dangerous because now the individual mistakenly assumes himself or herself to be walking a far superior path than before. Such individual, contrary to one's imagination, becomes far more rigid and ignorant towards finding out one's own weaknesses and mistakes because of the underlying confidence in having chosen a superior path of knowledge, wisdom, and spirituality. It is like choosing to share bed with your teenage daughter because letting your teenage son to do so is inappropriate.

In true sense, a sincere approach by any sane person to avoid the trap of choosing the worse alternative can be summarized in two steps. First, one should simply attempt to solve the current crisis. Second, one should not be in a hurry to pick another alternative. The only effort should be to stop. To Simply Stop. Once completely stopped, the mind becomes more open to make conscious decisions about the available alternatives. If a situation does not look favorable, we do not need to find all the answer right away. All we need to do is to stop. When we stop and look at a situation without trying to either solve it or get away from it, we do not fall in the trap of choosing worse alternative. It is only when we stop making decisions (whether running away from current situation or choosing an alternative one), we can find better solutions. These better solutions come up because we are able to perceive completely, without the unnecessary interruption from our mind or memory.

Our Limitations

Our physical limitation is the biggest hurdle in the way of total perception.

We never realize it, but the fact is that we are very much limited in how we perceive our world around us. This knowledge may come to us as a shock or a surprise. We may think how we can be called limited. We are the most superior of all races and animal kinds on this planet. We have created so much, invented so much, and controlled and managed everything around us. Yes, we have done quite a lot but still we should not forget that we have achieved all this despite our physical limitation. The limitation is quite simple and quite obvious, the limitation of observation. One cannot see oneself. It is against the nature of things to be able to perceive themselves. A knife cannot cut itself. An eye cannot see itself. An observe cannot observe itself. We see what our eyes show us. We hear what our ears make us hear. We are not made to doubt our own senses. We are what we perceive.

> *One aged husband asked a doctor for some medication for his wife as she seemed to be at loss of hearing. He gave him a box of pills and asked him to give her one pill everyday if she cannot hear from 30 feet away. He asked to give her two pills every day if she cannot hear from 20 feet away and to give her 3 pills every*

day if she cannot hear anything from 10 feet away. The husband went home and saw his wife cooking something in the kitchen with her back facing him. He called from outside and asked her what she was cooking. When he did not hear any response, he went to the door and asked her again. She seemed busy cooking without responding. He went near her and asked her again. She turned and said, "For the third time John, I said, I am cooking your favorite fried rice!"

This is what we do all the time. We perceive the world from our senses and our point of view. In our own view, we are perfect. That we perceive through our defective senses is interpreted as an imperfect entity because there is no way for us to figure out our own imperfection. When we are asked by the eye doctor to read the letters in front of us, we don't say that "the first letter is actually a 'Q' but I see it as a 'D'". We simply say that it is a 'D'. We always observe from the position of being right. We always argue believing that we are correct. This basic tendency of our minds is the root cause of all conflicts in the world. Not only we continue to defend our position, but we also hate all those who challenge our opinions, beliefs and reasonings. There is never a doubt that we are not right.

Our bodies have a physical existence in this world. We sense the universe around us through different sense organs. Each sense organ is an instrument allowing us to perceive special qualities of this universe such as sound, vision, taste, touch, and smell. Like every instrument, our sense organs also have their limitations. The ears can only hear sound within a specific range of frequencies. The nose, eyes and tongue also have their own limitations of how much they can sense. If some sensation lies outside the range of sense organs, we cannot ascertain their presence around us. What we do not see, do not hear, do not smell, or do not feel does not exist in our awareness. Besides all the physical senses, we also have a mind which creates thoughts and registers experiences as memories within our brains. Just like all physical sense organs, our minds too have become limited and confined into a closed unit captured by our ego, our thoughts, our memories and experiences, our culture, our social bonds, and our beliefs. It is almost impossible for most people to transcend any of our physical senses including the mind. With limited abilities to respond to the unlimited expanse of the universe, our wishes to be able to perceive our surroundings completely are far fetched.

The only sense we can transcend is the mind. All sense organs are an extension of the mind itself, and therefore, going above and beyond the limitations of the mind gives the necessary freedom to perceive the universe in its completeness. If we must transcend our limitations, we will have to change our affirmations from 'I am right' to 'I might be wrong.' The doubt that one could be wrong opens new possibilities. Such possibilities include enhanced wisdom, heightened perceptions and an incredibly receptive mind which is ready to embrace the higher dimension of our existence.

A Total Perception only is possible when
1. *You doubt your own intelligence before questioning others'.*
2. *Know that your physical form has its limitations.*
3. *Understand that you cannot ever perceive totally.*

Blind Following

Our blind faith in popular things and people make us blind to everything about them.

Mind is a very tricky instrument. We all are nothing but the slaves of the mind. When something happens repeatedly, it learns to adjust to it and then simply surrenders to give rise to a habit. Anything that becomes a habit is deeply rooted in the person's behavior. Soon, we get enslaved to those habits and follow all the routine maneuvers without needing to pay attention. Our biggest loss in following any of our habits is the missed opportunity of awareness. As long as we habitually function paying no attention, our sense organs continue to operate without our attention in registering those signals.

One of our habits is our mind's tendency to blindly follow famous people. We follow celebrities, successful and rich peoples, beautiful and influential ones. We very easily get influenced by anyone who has already influenced a large number of people. Once influenced with someone, we lose the ability to see, hear or notice anything completely. We believe everything they say, even if it might be the most ridiculous thing. We do not disbelieve, doubt, or even contradict anything such influential people say or do. We basically, shut our senses and ability to reason when it comes to interacting or even being in presence of our heroes, idols, icons, or superstars.

Our sense of perception is lost when we lose the ability to question, or reason about anything that we come across. The moment we accept something completely, our senses lose the power to present an alternative picture of the environment. This is why it is hard to question one's belief, one's culture, one's nationality, one's likes and dislikes and one's social, ethical, moral or religious values. If a strong nationalist looks at a picture of a flag, the sensation perceived by such a person will not be just of noticing a recognizable picture. Instead, it will be a strong sense of belongingness and pride. In nature, there is no real sensory signal that can be identified as pride or nationalism. It is just an illusory idea created and learned by the imagination of the mind. The same response is generated by people when it comes to following religious beliefs, cultural actions, ethical and moral values, or social biases. It must not be hard to believe that almost whole of the mankind at all the times and in all the areas is so heavily influenced by such habitual bounds of mind that there is no scope of perceiving any new information with a fresh perspective.

Blind Following damages our mind in the same manner, the mind, which is already made sluggish due to burden of practicing a belief system. People follow all kinds of famous people. When you follow someone, you completely surrender yourself. When you surrender, you surrender all your senses including the mind. In a surrendered state, the senses do not register, and the mind does not reason. In such a state, it is very difficult for people to be able to hear or read anything about their idol that does not match with their image. It is also difficult for such people to doubt anything that they say or suggest. If at all, they find anything they do not like, they simply ignore it and move on with their belief fully intact.

There are stories about the stupidity and illiteracy of Kalidas, the famous Indian poet of earlier centuries. Once he was picked by the priests and made to contest in a dual with the wisest one. The priests told Kalidas to be quiet and just answer with gestures. The wise one pointed up. Kalidas pointed down. The priests said that the wise one is saying that the God is up, looking at us while Kalidas is saying that the God is here right on this earth, in form of all living creatures. The wise one pointed one finger to which Kalidas pointed two fingers. The priests said that the wise one is saying that the God is One, while Kalidas says that the God is always accompanied by his other half such as Brahma with Saraswati, Shiva with Parvati and Vishnu with Laxmi. Lastly, the wise one showed open palm with five fingers to which Kalidas showed clenched fists. Priests said that the wise one is saying that there are five elements to which Kalidas is saying that there is only one Mind. People were thrilled. They believed that Kalidas was really very intelligent. Later the priests asked him what he meant by those gestures. Kalidas said that the wise one was trying to say that he would kick him up high in the sky so he tried to counter that he would push him down into the earth. He said that the wise one was trying to say that he would poke his finger into his eyes, so he wanted to poke both his fingers into his eyes. In the last when the wise one showed his open palm, he thought that the wise one was saying he would slap him so he said he would hit him back with fists.

We have already discussed about the nature of questions. When a person asks a question to another, it can be seen as non-acceptance of the latter's ideas, proposals or actions by the former. When you are influenced by someone, you do not and cannot doubt or ask questions. It is rude. If you ask a question, it is seen as a sign of disrespect. Even if the leader or the influencer understands that the question asked by someone from the crowd is genuinely for the purpose of getting clarity on an issue, most of the other followers will not appreciate it. The crowd always sees those asking questions as the rebellions and stops them by use of force. In the blind race to follow a leader, everyone looks at the others and tries to go with the flow, without doubting, resisting, or questioning.

What happens when you do not doubt or question something but simply go with the flow? You start believing everything that is presented to you because you see that millions of other people are already doing that. You do not want to believe that your doubts are valid when all others do not seem to have any problems. The mind loves repetitions and very soon finds itself comfortable in doing what it has always been doing on a regular basis. When we get a habit of following someone or something with our blind faith, we stop looking at it. We do not feel a need to check on things we would normally do with others. For example, if I have been using a toothpaste from Alexis company for many years, I will resist your giving me a different toothpaste when I come visit your home to stay for a night. I might as well need a lot of persuasion and validations from you about its qualities to finally accept it and use it. On the other hand, if you hand me a new kind of toothpaste which I never used in the past, but is made by the Alexis company, I will not even try to check if it's as good as I would like. My blind faith in someone or something will make me blind to all the future encounters. You might as well say that you stop perceiving when you are blindly following something or someone.

Blind Following makes you believe what the influential people want us to believe. Yet, it need not be only towards celebrities, most educated or the most famous people. It also works in the same dangerous manner for the language, clothing, mannerism, and countless other symbolic things that people have enslaved themselves to. Write or say anything strange, stupid, or unsubstantiated and use words like 'research', 'expert', 'science', or 'scientist' and people will believe it. Nobody will ever pause for a moment and try to question the validity of such statements because they have already put their blind faith into those powerful words. The reason why it is very easy to fool millions of people is because they are so predictable, they fall prey to such tactics repeatedly, without fail each time. Open any article, any news or any blog and you will notice the trick used repeatedly over time. Everything they want you to (blindly) believe is subtly interwoven with these words that shut your senses. Everything is research based. Every statement is made by scientists. Everything is based on science. The most amusing fact is that there are no two kinds of people, first those who are influencing and second those who are influenced. There are only one kind of people, and all of them are blind followers to something which could be influential people, processes, things, or ideas. One who can fool people into one kind of stupidity can be found easily influenced by somebody else in the game of stealing your common-sense from under your floor.

A Total Perception only is possible when
1. *We do not blindly follow anybody and are not afraid to question them or their actions before getting impressed with them.*
2. *We do not let our love or hate bind our senses.*

16

The Dual Mistake

We do not just do a mistake. We compound it by making another even bigger mistake.

When one wants to go dive deep into the nature of our mind and understand the realities of our true nature, even doing a single mistake proves to be expensive. The nature of duality of our minds makes it very difficult for us to come out of our limiting habits, rigid beliefs and mischievous tendencies acquired and accumulated over many years. The problem is that many times we do not just do a mistake. Instead, we do mistake in pairs, compounding the problem much more.

A total perception is not possible unless the mind and its tendencies are transcended. The mind tends to believe some things and disbelieve some other things. The tendencies to believe or not to believe makes our minds very rigid and unable to perceive our world in its original state. Such a mind tends to pay more attention to things that align with its beliefs and ignore those things that oppose its belief system. It is fairly common to see the mind's tendency to do mistake in pairs. It does not simply do a mistake, but instead, compounds its effects by going a step further and adding another layer of mistake. This compounding nature of mind's doing mistakes is the main reason why it is not easy for people to come out of the trap of ignorance.

If a mind must perceive totally, it must start letting go its habits which stops it from doing it so. Let us understand what a compounded mistake is. Assume there is a person who believes in wrong ideas. If you were to help this person, you would try to help him feed more and more of good ideas, so that the strength of good ideas slowly and effectively flush the bad ideas out of his or her mind. This is fairly reasonable! If a person is just watching one news channel, he or she forms an opinion based on that channel's views. If the channel is biased towards one particular issue, the person knows only those issues. If on the other hand, you make him view five more channels, the varying opinions on different channels will slowly flush out the wrong views from the person's mind. A compounding mistake happens when that the person is not only believing in wrong ideas but at the same time, is also disbelieving right ideas. This is an impossible situation! This means that the person is not interested in viewing any other channel. What can you do with this person? Whatever good ideas you want to feed, the person is already opposing and resisting them. Moreover, the person continues to get engaged with bad ideas. Can you see the trap of the Dual or Compounded Mistakes? A person not only believes that his religion is the only right one and his God is the only right God, but he or she also believes that all other religions are not good, or their God is not the real God. This is why it is impossible to make a highly religious person to come out of his or her belief system or even discuss about any conflicting views.

We have already talked about how we miss reality (by failing to perceive totally) because we follow them blindly whom we know are influential, powerful, and resourceful. The compounding mistake happens because not only we are only paying attention to the rich, famous, and influential people but we are also ignoring or escaping all other things which are poor, ordinary, and insignificant (in our view). This dual-pair mistake makes it impossible to perceive completely. How can it? We ourselves are ensuring that we will not observe anything that we do not find important. If we have already made up our mind about the whole universe what is worth perceiving and what is not, then why even the God would bother changing our views? Had we done only one mistake and followed everybody blindly, we might have noticed something worthwhile at sometimes from someone. We might also have had some chance to get a total perception at a few moments if we had not cared to believe anyone, however influential, powerful, or resourceful. Any one of the mistakes was far less damaging in terms of our perceiving capability, but both of them together make it almost impossible for us to get any help.

How would you tame a mind which is not only looking at the wrong source of knowledge but also giving a blind eye to the right source of knowledge? It is far easier to make some progress if the mind was looking at the wrong knowledge only, because then some chances of it at looking at a right knowledge too existed. Once the mind starts looking at the right knowledge, its ability to figure out right from wrong might help it further identify the wrong knowledge on its own. Things are far more complicated because the mind not only has a way towards wrong knowledge or idea, but also has itself completely turned off from the right knowledge or idea.

Security

Our insecurities, fear and need to hold on to some anchor makes it impossible for us to perceive completely.

We are insecure. We are always looking for security, safety, and predictability in our lives. This deep-rooted need of safety in evident in every little action of ours whether done intentionally or ignorantly. This habit affects and guides all our actions, choices, and expectations. This is the way nature has designed us - as fearful entities. It is only reasonable that unless the creatures are fearful of their safety and existence, they will not protect themselves or their young ones to survive and to grow on to continue thriving on this planet.

Our need for security manifests in many ways. One of our insecurities is found in the form of end goals. We do not want to pursue any task if we are not sure where it leads us. Whenever we encounter a situation where we have to act on something, our first question is 'why'? If I ask a person to dig a hole in the ground, he will need to know why he must do the job. It can either be a job which pays him money, or it can be a way of punishment which he finds himself being forced into. In no case a person would be at ease doing something with no knowledge about its purpose. The very fact that someone starts on the path of spirituality is because of the deep-rooted urge to know about the purpose of the life itself. Absence of a reason or the end goal of any activity makes one feel very insecure. It gives them a feeling as if they are walking an unknown path with no idea about its direction or the dangers in the way. A sense of purpose, even if it is totally false and made up, provides the much-needed security to the restless mind.

There is another form of security that we look for in our lives. We find great comfort in methods, processes, and directions. In absence of a knowledge about how to go about certain activity, we find ourselves helpless and greatly insecure. If I am asked to walk in a dark and unknown place, my insecurity and uncertainty will make it very difficult for me. On the contrary, if the place is dark but a known place, I will have the security of the past knowledge of the place and would not feel as much uncertainty as I would find at a totally unknown place. In such places such as my home where I live, I would walk in the dark along the terrains from my memory of the past experiences with the place. On the other hand, if the place is unknown, I might find insecurity even during a daytime because it is not just the terrain, but all other unknown facts about the place which make me feel insecure.

One of the most crucial form of insecurity in all of us is about our future. We fear of the times when there might not be sufficient food or shelter for us. We want to ensure a continuous supply of life's essential things for us to reduce pain and suffering. It is this very uncertainty that forces us to live in fear. We are fearful of losing our jobs, we are fearful of losing our loved ones and we are fearful of losing our health. If it is not the pain in the current times, we are fearful of a possible pain in the unseen future. Being afraid of the unknown future, we continue to look for securing it by accumulating as much as we can to survive the times when there is not much food, resources, or comforts. In this struggle to be safe and secure, we continue to live the life feeling insecure all our life and afraid of letting go everything we possess.

> *Two teachers were walking down a road when one said to other, "If I have all the wealth of Bill Gates, I will be richer than he is right now." The other asked how was that possible. The teacher said, "Because, I will have my monthly $1500 from the two tuitions."*

Spirituality is about existing in the world as it is and not how it should be. The reality is that there is no safety in this universe. Our future is always going to be uncertain no matter how much prepared we are towards achieving certainty. Yet, our expectations are to be safe and remain so for eternity. This approach of looking at every phenomenon in terms of its future certainty or uncertainty makes us miss the present moment and we continue to observe our universe with the eyes of the mind. Our minds do not register things as they are, but they look at the things as they should be.

> *A Total Perception only is possible when*
> 1. *We realize that there is no absolute security in life.*

The Maya

Is it our incomplete perception that makes us believe our world as real or is the illusory nature of our world that gives us incomplete perception?

When you encounter a copy, image, reflection, or a replica of something, how do you look at it? If you happen to visit Eiffel Tower in Paris, you will find individuals selling keychains with a tiny replica of the Eiffel Tower. When you see such models, how do you observe them? What qualities do you look in them? If I ever gave you a tiny model of Taj Mahal, one of the seven wonders of the world, what would you look in it? Would you attempt to analyze its design and comment if it should not contain a round top or that the number of towers surrounding it should not be four but should be some other number? Even if you suggest that it should have been made in a certain material or made of certain color, you know it very well that you are not trying to alter the design and shape of the original Taj Mahal, but are referring to an image of the original. You know that there is nothing that you can do to this image or the replica that can affect the original, the real Taj Mahal.

When you hear someone singing a famous song, how do you hear it? When you appreciate the singing what do you appreciate? Do you appreciate the content, tune, lyrics, or the length of the song? Or do you appreciate how well the song was sung like the original one? When you do not like this song, what is it that you do not like? Is it ever about the content, tune, or lyrics? Whenever you hear a copy or replica of a known song, the content, tune, lyrics, or any other feature still belong to the original. Any comments you make about these qualities still refer to the original. When hearing such song sung by someone, if you say that you do not like the lyrics, you are not complaining about the copy but the original song. The comments on the current singer can only be limited to how close it resembles is with the original. Knowing the real and the replica or image helps you in a big way about where to focus your attention. A copy can only be blamed for its accuracy of closeness with the real. Every other attribute observed in a copy belongs to the original.

We very well understand that we behave differently when we encounter something original as opposed to when we face an imitation or a reflection of something original. When we interact with something original, we are aware that the original object or a thing is an embodiment of all its qualities and characteristics. It is responsible for everything good as well as everything bad about it. If I look at a rose, then I am aware of the reality of the rose and its fragrance as well as the thorns associated with it. A rose in reality, comprises of everything associated with it, such as its name, form, interpretations, and associations. On the other hand, if I look at an imitation of a rose, such as a rose made of plastic, I do not expect it to have fragrance or be surrounded with bees or butterflies. I do not pay attention to its color, shape or size except from the angle of accurateness of imitation. The only thing anyone would ever look in an imitation is its similarity or dissimilarity with the original. Except for that one quality, no one is interested in an imitation on any other issue.

> *A movie named Arjun Reddy was a huge success in South India. As the trend goes, the maker of the film recreated the movie in different language with different actors and actresses. The movie recreated was not a separate movie in real sense, it was a copy, a recreation. In North India, hardly anyone had seen the original movie. All the discussions, disputes, comments and criticism about the story and its presentation in the North India were targeted to the remake version named as Kabir Singh.*

The only purpose an imitation serves is to represent another object or idea. The only observation one can or must make about such replicas is about the closeness in resemblance with the original. This is the only purpose of an image or a reflection. When we look in the mirror and make a comment about the looks of our hair, or the appropriateness of our dress, we are not commenting on the image, but are referring to the direct reality, ourselves. In the same manner, when we look at a model, all our comments about its shape or quality is referred to the object that it points to. When we look at a model of Taj Mahal and say that it should have gotten ten towers around it, we are trying to say it for the original Taj Mahal and not the model. We know it very well that the model must be an exact replica of the original and we would not make a mistake of changing the model while leaving the original untouched.

Have we ever thought what exactly is our world? Is it as real as it looks or is it a reflection of something else? Are we sure that our world is a reality? What if what we see is not the reality but a reflection of our way of looking, observing, perceiving, or interpreting it? What happens if we take a reflection as an original by mistake? If you took the key ring as a real Eiffel Tower, would your assessment of the Eiffel Tower be correct or even close to reality? Can you ever know about the real Eiffel Tower if all you can observe is a little key ring? How close is the reality to the reflection of the reality? How close is a real Taj Mahal to the model of Taj Mahal that you hold in the palms of your hands?

If you encounter some ancient sacred scriptures who mention that the world is nothing but an illusion, what will be your reaction? If some knowledgeable person went on preaching about the limitation of our perceptions and the illusory nature of the universe, would you not want to stop how you have been living so far and start thinking if it would be right to continue living (in the same ignorant manner) without first ensuring if this is really the case? What is on stake if we were wrong so far and the world was actually a reflection in our consciousness and not the reality as we took it so far? What is at stake here? Do we care to find out?

A Total Perception only is possible when
  1. *We are able to separate the Real from the Imitation.*

Ego

Strong belief in one's own beliefs makes it impossible to perceive any differently.

We all have a complete faith in our own beliefs, rationale, decisions, and our ways of behaving. Everybody operates from the stand of 'I am right'. It is very hard and painful for someone to accept a mistake or a mistaken point of view.

Listen to a kid trying to explain something to its mom. If the mother tries to advice, correct or counter argue, the kid will still continue to operate from the standpoint that its action is right, and it is the mother who is failing to understand. "Mom, you don't understand," is their favorite reply. Listen to an employee talking about his Boss. There is no single person in this world who agrees with his boss when he or she is denied a good review or a decent increment. It is not in our genes to accept a fault and let the other party win without our attempting to put our version of truth. The same is the case for every supervisor too. There is no Boss in this world, who would say that his decisions to fire someone, or to deny someone a promotion or his criteria or work allotment to his subordinates is wrong. No kid is wrong, no parent is wrong.

No Boss or a subordinate is wrong. Nobody is ever wrong. This is what we are. We operate from the position of, "I am right."

With our ego confident of itself as being right all the times, we continue to live every aspect of our lives with the same conviction. We are proud of everything of ours, which could be our beliefs, our values, our culture, our kids, our decisions, our religion, and our habits. If I am a Christian, I am always going to look at any religious act from the point of a Christian. I may pretend to look interested in listening or knowing about other religions, but in my heart, I know that the Jesus is the only real God. It is like someone might be respectful to other people's parents, yet their dad or mom is the best! We not only just believe but instead have a firm conviction that our values and culture are the best. If I am raised as a vegan, I feel that being vegan is a supreme habit and I take a great pride in my habit. Later in the life, if I chose not to be a vegan, I still continue to be proud of my new choices. I am always right. If I was not eating meat, it was the best habit. If I am now eating meat, it is still the best habit. I was right then. I am right now. Even though, I may continue to change my own priorities and habits and my opinions over the life a few thousand times, I still know that I have been right in each one of those decisions. How strange is that!

What does this behavior pattern of the ego do to our mindset? Can we ever undergo a radical transformation in our lives which must include a change in the way we think, perceive, or do different acts? Let us forget a radical transformation, can we even change a little bit while we remain addicted to the idea of being right at all the time? Who has more chance to improve and grow, one who knows his or her mistakes or the one who knows that he or she is always right?

Those who have had a little exposure to spirituality and started looking at different scriptures or listened to wise ones know that the ego needs to be destroyed completely for the wisdom to be revealed. This is our problem. Who would be the one to destroy the ego? Would it be anyone other than the ego itself? We are asking for a situation where the ego who always knows that it is right, starts accepting that everything about it is wrong. This is a wishful thinking! It is like expecting that the fire becomes cooler and the ice becomes warmer. It can simply not happen. A cool fire is no fire. A warm ice is not ice, it is water. An ego cannot accept that it is not right. It is like a death to the ego. Nobody wants to die. Each one of us, including every other creature in this universe, is programmed to avoid pain and death. Likewise, an ego will never operate from the position of being wrong.

> *There used to be an old woman in a village who had a rooster. The old lady believed that it was the rooster who made the sun rise in the village by crowing every morning and used to fight the villagers everyday about it. The villagers got fed up and finally asked her to leave the village. The old woman took her rooster and moved to another village. The next morning, the rooster crowed, and the sun rose. The lady smiled and said, "Let those villagers suffer because there won't be any sunrise in their village."*

The strong belief of ego in its own belief presents a great barrier towards gaining a reasonable insight into the nature of things, knowledge, and wisdom. Without change in the way we perceive the world around ourselves, a real transformation is not possible for us. A change in the way we perceive cannot happen unless we realize that we are not perceiving the world in right way. The ego is not designed to come to such a realization that it needs to change the way it perceives, interprets, or understands the world currently. The result is that we continue to exist in this world of ignorance despite our countless attempts to change our ways. It is not surprising to see that millions of people in the world have been subscribing to yoga, meditation, spirituality camps, reading scriptures and practicing religion, and yet hardly a handful end up gaining the real wisdom.

> *A Total Perception only is possible when*
>   *1. We doubt our own beliefs.*

Impatience

Our failure to stay in the moment makes us lose what is available to our senses right now.

Mind is slippery. It is almost impossible to keep it focused. It tends to shift attention at the very next opportunity it finds. Unless one is extremely attentive and committed to remain at a single point, the mind would continue to shift from place to place unhindered. Please understand that this 'commitment' is not a strongly enforced action such as a regular practice or meticulously laid out plans. Instead, it is a subtle intent that continues to fill your background at all the times. This attentiveness can be compared with a mother who is busy doing various activities all day and is still attentive to a slightest sound or movement in her baby in the house.

Let us try to understand what is being said here. We have already discussed that our minds are always moving either to reduce pain or to increase pleasure. This is not an opinion; this is a simple truth. When something is observed, an evaluation is made about the nature of the thing. If the thing seems to add to possible pleasure, the mind desires acquiring it. On the other hand, if the thing seems possibly dangerous, lethal or to cause pain, the mind wishes to keep itself away from it. If it is neither, then the mind gets bored and gets distracted to some other movement. The mind continues to operate like this every second, every minute and every day of its entire life. It is this very nature of the mind (of viewing the world through the lens of pleasure and pain) that stops it from simply observing anything without getting into the trap of acquiring or relinquishing it if it is found worth observing.

Let us imagine a situation involving you where something went wrong. Very soon you find your close friends and well-wishers trying to explain where in this situation you might have gone wrong. You cannot stay with the fact that that someone else is pointing out your mistake. You start with trying to avoid this situation (where you feel uncomfortable about a possible mistake on your part and the pain of having to face it). You resort to rationalizing your behavior and to explain why you did what you did. You believe that your acts were perfect, and the mistakes would not have happened if certain things did not happen the way they did. The present scenario is so painful that you cannot stand the burden of being (proven) wrong. You do all possible efforts to run out of this situation. As we said, it is the nature of the mind to avoid pain and suffering. The idea does not appear to your mind that your friends might possibly want you to observe the situation so completely that the mistake on your part becomes a learning experience and makes you handle such situations in future with more maturity. It is a simple fact that when you fail to remain with a moment, you cease to notice what went wrong. Having lost an opportunity to absorb the current experience completely in our consciousness, we continue to repeat the same mistakes in future. It is a common understanding that practice makes perfect and people learn from their own mistakes and grow on to become more mature with time. The reality is that we run away once again when we face the similar situation where we might be a party in the things gone wrong. We fail to learn this time too just like any other time. We go on escaping all conflicting situations and avoiding any discussion or analysis to remain 'safe'. If only we were attentive, we could notice the patterns of mistakes repeating and our not learning from our past experiences. This little attention itself could make us pay attention to our mistake in present time and add this learning to our growing wisdom. Yet, most conveniently, when our friends and well-wishers bring us back the memory of similar experience of past so that we could at least pay attention and learn this time, we hate our friends and well-wishers for bringing us the (painful) memory of our past mistake. We take it as their idea of making fun of us, trying to demean us, push us down, insult us and prove to us that we are not worthy. Therefore, we miss the moment again (and the friends). First time, we tried to avoid looking at our mistake and try to think how it could be avoided. Second time onwards, we try to avoid looking at (the memory of) it again because it brings us painful memories of the past too! There is no way one could come out of this never-ending trap of avoiding looking at the painful moments which are either of the past or of the present.

There are some other ways too in which we fail to stay with the moment. In some cases, when we do not like someone, we simply do not notice anything they do however worthwhile it might be. Instead, we try to find possible faults or mistakes on their part. We do not pay attention in hate. We do not pay attention in love too. If we love someone, we fail to notice any mistake with the person. If we are watching our little daughter perform on the stage, we are going to be totally in love with her performance. It is possible that nobody else in the audience find the performance any interesting. It is possible that she made many mistakes, but we would never know.

It is not only the conflicts that we tend to avoid in present moment. In fact, we miss the present moment at all the times. Our world is becoming more and more busy with actions, tasks, responsibilities, and goals. Everyone is loaded with many burdens and we hardly find time to relax the mind. Our minds are full of thoughts. These thoughts contain memory of our past experiences, good and bad ones, as well as worries of expectations from future events. If we have an inventory of unfulfilled tasks to attend sometime in the next moment, hour, day, week, month, year, or many years, we are going to miss what is going around us. One misses what is near if one looks far. Therefore, most adults have lost smile from their faces. They are busy thinking, planning, and executing and therefore, missing the magic around them. They miss their little daughter's laughter, they miss their wife's beauty, they miss the bird's playful singing in the morning, and they miss a few hundred of such magical moments every day of their lives.

We fail to stay with the moment in love and hate, in busy times where we are thinking of past or worrying about future, or when we are trying to overcome our insecurities. This means that there are hardly any times when we are not involved in one or more of such actions. To stay with the moment is almost an impossible task. One can neither come to the present moment consciously nor can one come to it unconsciously. It will not be an easy task for the human mind to overcome this behavior.

A Total Perception only is possible when
 1. *We fail to look at a conflict whole-heartedly.*
 2. *We fail to look at our patterns of avoiding conflicts.*

21

Stubbornness

We continue doing the same things that never worked in the past.

The world is changing every moment. Those who are not attentive will miss most of the magic. The attention is not a matter of focusing on something of interest. An attention is a matter of being open to everything, to the whole universe. To be open to the universe around us means not only to allow the necessary freedom to your sense organs but also to let the (restless) mind to become quiet and the habits and conditionings to slow down. The sad reality is that most people continue to exist on this planet in a survival mode. Their behavior is driven by the basic tendencies of the senses and their minds are trapped in the prison of their insecurities while they continue to chase their never-ending desires.

There are certain actions that at certain times may lead us to success and other times, those same actions may be the reason for our failures. An ignorant person is one who does not know when a certain habit can work to one's advantage and when it becomes a burden. Such people habitually tend to repeat actions that never worked in past. The habit of repetition is usually seen as desirable positive quality and called with different names such as persistence, determination, or endurance. People admire those who continue to work on the same thing with a complete determination to achieve some goal. However, this attitude of relentlessly pursuing something using the same methods repeatedly despite facing failures is one of the reasons why we continue to shut most of our senses and greatly limit our perceptions.

There is a story of a person who decided to dig a well because he had to walk a long way to collect water from the nearby village. It is said that when he spent a few days digging about forty feet with no sight of water, he stopped digging in frustration and went a little farther to start digging a new hole. In the next few days he dug another forty or fifty feet and found no water. He abandoned that too and started digging at a new place a little away from there. It is said that he was never found water because he never dug deep enough at any one place.

Stories like these try to push this idea in the minds that it is always stupid to go on changing your decision and moving on if something did not work in your favor. This is ridiculous! If the oil companies started taking such advice, they might go out of business. It is true that they have to try a number of attempts to figure out which site will provide a better yield of oil. The earth is not same everywhere. At some place there might be no water even hundred feet below and within a kilometer, you might find water at fifty feet depth. There are some places where there are hard rocks beneath the surface and there are other places where the earth is porous. You cannot make standard rules in life based on one single example. An intelligent person decides when to continue and when to drop out based on the situation and examining one's own position in that situation.

Our minds are very rigid, hardened, and adamant. When something does not work in the initial attempts, the mind cannot easily accept defeat. It thinks that if the act were pursued with more aggression, vigor and energy, maybe the results would come out different. This habit (of the mind) is deeply rooted in each one of us. Whether it is a two-year-old child or a seventy-year-old mature human, they both can be seen frustratingly trying to do some impossible act repeatedly for a long time.

I saw my wife trying to push a drawer. The drawer went in halfway and then got stuck somewhere. She pulled it out and pushed it again, a bit harder this time. The drawer got stuck in the same position as before. She went on and continued to try pushing it at least five-six more times, each time giving it a harder push.

We all do this. We tend to think that somehow something would fix itself if we pursued enough. When something gets stuck, we try harder. Repeating an action once might make sense because many times things do get sorted in a repeated attempt. But when things do not work the second time, we do not stop and pause for a moment to give it a break and to see what we are doing. Instead, we continue to increase our efforts doing it in the exact same manner without any sign of attempting a different approach.

It seems this habit originates from our tendencies to stick with the *known*. We find security in what we know. It is unsafe to try new approach or walk a new path or attempt a new process. We all fear uncertainties and try to prefer a certain approach against an uncertain one. Even if it is a simple matter of pushing a drawer, all we know is to push it. Therefore, if pushing it first time does not work, we do not know anything else besides pushing it harder the next time. Our tendency to stick with the known also limits our expanse of creativity. When trying to find something, we continue to search not only those places where we think we might have lost it but also in the same ways that we have tried multiple times already.

> *My daughter was frustrated for the last thirty minutes. She was trying to look for her phone which she thought she must have left at the couch where she was studying the previous night. Besides the couch, she also looked at two other places where she normally keeps it. She kept coming back to the couch, and tried flipping the pillow, the sheet, and the books a few hundred times in a hope to find the phone. She tried calling the number, but it was not much help because she usually kept the phone in silent mode. At last, seeing her try the same way for so long, I got up and suggested that she tried something different. I closed the curtains, switched the lights off and made the room completely dark and asked her to call her phone again. The moment she dialed the number, her phone could be seen underneath the couch with its screen lightened up.*

To repeat is the nature of the mind. In the process of improving upon everything that we do, the mind tends to make use of our memories and past experiences to decide how it acts in the future. It is always safer to go with the known and therefore repeating an act comes naturally (to the mind). The problem with working with a mind conditioned to act in a known way is that we can never look at anything freshly because once known, we continue to look at the things with our past experiences (with them). If one must perceive the universe freshly at every moment, one will need to let go the tendency of the mind to behave in its routine and repetitive manner. One would need to forget all that one knows in order to know something fresh.

It is one thing to be completely unaware and to repeat the same unyielding efforts whenever stuck in some situation, but it is completely different thing to avoid any outside help to accept change. When someone else sees us stuck in a rut and tries to come up with some suggestions and offers some changes in our lifestyle, we resist with full force. Nobody likes others telling them what to do if stuck. It is felt as an insult. It seems to them that if they accepted those changes, their weaknesses would be revealed, and their attempts would be proven wrong. The mind always wants to be proven right. If shown otherwise, it will justify why it is right and why no change is needed.

> *Whenever I meet my father, he complains about some issues and some problems he is facing. But the moment I come up with some suggestions thinking that it might help him solve his problems, he changes the topic. He said he does not want me to suggest solutions. He simply wants me to hear his problems.*

A repeating mind is unaware, non-receptive and completely blind. It is not ready to perceive. It is not ready to change. It is not ready to grow. There is practically no hope. If we pay some serious attention and look at our underlying subtle behavior, we will find that our whole life is happening in the same mode. It is a mere repetition. Look at any one day of our life and try to see if it is any different than the previous day. Have we not reacted the same way to some teasing, some complains, some abuses, some praises, and some argument? He we not carried out all the activities of this day with the same routine as any other day where we have dreamed for some unfulfilled wishes, carried out the same routine tasks and talked about the same topics that we have discussed a few hundred times in the past? Do we do anything different any day? Can we even think of doing things differently at all? How can we, unless we stop doing what we are doing and see what we are doing to our lives? Are we not simply living life in our dreams? The truth is that we are not even awake. We might be awake in worldly sense, but our actions can clearly show us that we are asleep, habitually repeating our actions as we continue to live day after day.

> *A Total Perception only is possible when*
> 1. *We become aware that we repeat our actions without awareness.*

SUMMARY

Total Perception is possible only when:

1. We drop our habit to exist in survival mode (Chasing Happiness and Avoiding Pain).
2. We drop fear of that which is new and uncertain.
3. We face opposing point of view in the same way as we face approvals and acceptance.
4. We observe without memory.
5. We observe only with our senses, not our brain.
6. We are not eager to reach somewhere.
7. We are not eager to get something, drop something or finish something.
8. We do not give too much value to experiences.
9. We stop trying to 'know.'
10. We stop taking interest in the story behind real life events.
11. We do not have a strong sense of identification.
12. We feel pain for every living creature.
13. We love everything in this universe in the same way.
14. We stop looking and interpreting life with rational mind.
15. We look at what is and not what must be.
16. We do not run away from criticism or exposing our weaknesses.
17. We do not just behave as how the society wants us to behave.
18. We try to please others.
19. We are not doing multiple tasks.
20. We are not thinking or past or planning for future.
21. We are not unduly busy with useless activities.
22. We stop behaving based on our preconceived notions.
23. We are able to look anything new without a prior knowledge.
24. We embrace uncertainty wholeheartedly.
25. We embrace, "I do not know" approach

26. We do not remain stuck to bad or good experiences.
27. We are not resisting questions and problems.
28. We are comfortable with questions and not necessarily trying to find answers for every question.
29. When we start questioning everyone and everything.
30. We become aware of who we are.
31. We are comfortable with the unknown and uncertain.
32. We are comfortable with letting go.
33. We understand that there is no real security in life Ever.
34. We are able to notice warning signs.
35. We can notice the weaknesses of the Mind to fall for bold and beautiful and go beyond it.
36. You are aware that there are no material rewards in the end.
37. You are left with absolutely no expectations or hope.
38. You doubt your own intelligence before questioning others'.
39. Know that your physical form has its limitations.
40. Understand that you cannot ever perceive totally.
41. We do not blindly follow anybody and are not afraid to question them or their actions before getting impressed with them.
42. We do not let our love or hate bind our senses.
43. If we are sure that we are not focusing on something that is not real.
44. If we are comfortable waiting.
45. If we stop doing what we are doing occasionally and notice ourselves.
46. If we can surprise ourselves on regular basis by doing something for the first time.
47. We realize that there is no absolute security in life.
48. When we are able to separate the Real from the Imitation.

49. We become aware that we repeat our actions without awareness.
50. We doubt our own beliefs.
51. We could look at a conflict whole-heartedly.
52. We could look at our patterns of avoiding conflicts.